BARN in the U.S.A.

BARN in the U.S.A.

Bob Crittendon

Fulcrum Publishing
Golden, Colorado

Library of Congress Cataloging-in-Publication Data
Crittendon, Robert.
  Barn in the U.S.A. / Bob Crittendon.
      p. cm.
  Includes bibliographical references.
  ISBN-13: 978-1-55591-560-5 (pbk.)
  ISBN-10: 1-55591-560-4 (pbk.)
  1. Barns--United States--History. 2. Vernacular architecture--United States--History. I. Title: Barn in the United States of America. II. Title.
  NA8230.C75 2006
  728'.9220973--dc22
                          2006005684

ISBN-13: 978-1-55591-560-5
ISBN-10: 1-55591-560-4

Printed in China by P. Chan & Edward, Inc.
0 9 8 7 6 5 4 3 2

Design: Jack Lenzo
Editorial: Faith Marcovecchio, Katie Raymond
Graphics coordination: Ted Studley
Assignment photos: Jim Youden
Barn illustrations: Henry Studley

Fulcrum Publishing
16100 Table Mountain Parkway, Suite 300
Golden, Colorado 80403
(800) 992-2908 • (303) 277-1623
www.fulcrumbooks.com

This book is respectfully dedicated to all preservationists who share a reverence for irreplaceable things, such as these beloved old barns. Your example has fueled our interest and encouraged us throughout this project. With special thanks, too, to Jim Youden, whose back roads photo treks captured many rare barn images for all of us to enjoy.

Contents

Introduction

I recall as a boy five years of age first setting foot in my grandfather's barn in Martin, Tennessee. As it turned out, that was the only time I ever visited the family farm, but my mental picture of that old barn is as crisp and clear today as if it were only yesterday … so clear, in fact, that it stands out as one of the few indelible images of my boisterous boyhood. I've often mused over that memory and why an initial encounter with a piece of rural architecture should leave such a deep and long-lasting impression. Perhaps you've felt some of the same feelings and harbored some of the same curiosity.

For me, I have concluded that there is no single reason for my attachment. It is likely a synthesis of several logical and sensory inputs. First, the barn's size bowled me over, and for a five-year-old, everything looks pretty big. I was accustomed to smaller houses, small rooms, and low ceilings. To me, this was a huge, cathedral-like building. More important, it was a huge and unknown building, with unexplored dark corners. There was a mystery about it that captivated me. And, for a boy whose only pet was a small dog, it held another lure: there were big farm animals that were there or that had been there. To cement all those seen and unseen attractions, there were the other sensory seducements: the sounds of pigeons in the loft, the sweet fragrance of hay, and the leathery smells of harnesses and horse collars. I was hooked.

That image from long ago is a big part of the reason why I wanted to do this book. My experience is not unlike many others'—probably you included—who have a soft spot for barns. Barns have been described as American icons, and they are undeniably the most dominant landmark on the rural landscape. But I think their description as a "bridge to the past" is more germane. The traditional big red barn represents a connection to a better time, or at least to an era we recall as having bedrock values and simple, straightforward honesty, morality, and goodness. We associate the barn and the family farm with earlier, better days … days when kids climbed trees and going to town seemed like really going somewhere. Evenings when we caught lightning bugs in a jar, and when it got later, the family spent time together—even if it was just sitting around listening to the radio. It's not surprising that the sight of a barn awakens those good, nostalgic feelings, just as the sight of a weathered and abandoned old country church may uncomfortably suggest a sagging spiritual condition in the land.

The other thing driving a "barn book" was more reverential. We wanted to pay our respects to barns in general, but more particularly to those historic and unusual structures (many of them still standing today) that set the standards for others to follow. It is important to share their pictures and to tell their stories. So, as much as possible, we dug out the real history and real people behind each. Admittedly, details on architectural principles and construction detail were slighted—other texts are available to supply that. Nor is this a *Guinness* book: we were not searching for the biggest or the smallest barn or the

Opposite: 1870s Lewis family barn on Valley Road, Reno, Nevada. © Photo by Jack Hursh

most decorated. We also resisted the temptation to show a lot of pretty pictures of anonymous barns with no clue as to where they are, who created them, or what ordeals they survived. Our hope is that we tell readers enough of the story behind each barn without telling you more than you wanted to know.

Finally, a word of explanation: why western barns? To begin with, because there are far fewer of them than in the barn-rich country of the Midwest and northeastern United States—and they are more diverse in many ways, because the geography and weather conditions are so different. Another more compelling reason to focus on barns of the West, though, is that the small original base of barns is disappearing at a much faster pace than elsewhere. We wanted to show you the *best* historic western barns before they became the *only* historic western barns. The century-old barn that is a valuable historic treasure is too often knocked down to make way for a new shopping center. Soon they may all be gone. In Southern California, for example, only a handful of historic barns remain—and there are new generations of schoolchildren who may describe something as being "big as a barn," but who may have never actually seen a barn.

Horse at Rancho Los Alamitos, Long Beach, California.

Wagon wheel at Cook barn, San Juan Capistrano, California.

For years, we have enjoyed these enduring structures, marveled at their beauty and grace, and said, "If these barns could talk!" Well, now we think they have. If you agree and find this book worthwhile and enjoyable reading, we will consider the work a success. If it helps increase public awareness and serves the cause of barn preservation, we will be more than pleased. We applaud the National Trust for Historic Preservation and all other preservationists for helping to "preserve and protect the irreplaceable." These great old barns are an important national heritage that must not be consigned to oblivion.

—Bob Crittendon

Opposite: Dogie Jones's 1913 barn in Watrous, New Mexico.

Where Vaqueros Rode:
Rancho Los Alamitos, Long Beach, California

You can almost hear the long-distant hoofbeats when you walk through the gates of Rancho Los Alamitos in Long Beach, California. Alamitos (which means "little cottonwood trees") was once a busy working ranch with cultivated fields and livestock. Originally a 300,000-acre land grant awarded in 1790 to a Spanish foot soldier, Manuel Nieto, the holdings were quickly reduced in a land dispute with Mission San Gabriel and further diminished in 1806 when Nieto's heirs split the land into five ranches.

One of those, the 28,500-acre Rancho Los Alamitos, became an outpost ranch of Nieto's eldest son, Juan Jose. This windswept mesa was home to three generations of hard-riding vaqueros until acquired by John Bixby in 1878. Bixby, who built the first barn here in 1882, raised trotting carriage horses, and his son Fred later raised Belgian draft horses and the taller, showy shires. Alamitos also became a finishing ranch for cattle and the headquarters for other Bixby ranches. The barns that housed Bixby's horses and cattle here were all well designed and well built, most with Northern California redwood or lodgepole pine.

By the 1900s, however, the passage from ranching to urbanization was accelerating and the open ranchland was shrinking. In the late 1960s, the Bixby descendants gave the remaining estate, gardens, and six great barns to the city of Long Beach as a cultural and educational facility. The mild western weather near the Southern California coast has been gentle to the barns over the years, and they are in prime condition in this beautiful ranch park.

There is a seeming incongruity to horse barns and palm trees existing side by side, only a few miles from the ocean. But contrast and change come naturally to this land, which has seen the wheel turn from early Indian villages to survival under the Spanish, Mexican, and American flags. Fortunately, the barns and home exist today, open to the public, as a valuable reminder of that storied past.

This handsome horse barn replaced the original 1882 structure, which was destroyed by fire in 1947.

The dairy barn loft has worn well and is still very serviceable, despite its advanced age.

The big stallion barn is one of five barns encircling a grassy area for showing the horses.

Opposite: The saltbox-style 1909 dairy barn remains in pristine condition.

Built by the Buckaroos:
Peter French Round Barn, Harney County, Oregon

When poet Sam Walter Foss exhorted, "Give me men to match my mountains," he could have been talking about Peter French. French was small in size (five foot, five inches), but a bigger-than-life Oregon cattle king, developer, and land baron, dreamer, schemer, and barn builder. He lived a colorful life that began in 1849 and ended the day after Christmas in 1897 when he was shot to death by an irate homesteader. What he left behind is a sizeable niche in Oregon history and a historic 1880s round barn that today draws barnophiles from all over the country.

The energetic young man came to southeastern Oregon at age twenty-four to buy grazing land. He found plenty in Blitzen Valley and eventually would hold 200,000 acres, including a dozen ranches, a large mansion, and other buildings that he built as head-quarters for his "P" Ranch. At its peak, Peter French's ranching operation was one of the largest holdings in the West, encompassing several hundred employees, 45,000 cattle, and 3,000 horses and mules.

He was idolized by his cowboys and had distinguished himself in early clashes with raiding Indians. But he was also an aggressive empire builder and tangled repeatedly with settlers over boundaries and water rights. When the government promoted settlement in the area in 1880, French angered many with his tactics for acquiring land under the marshland rule, and a classic pro-cattle Big Rancher versus Small Homesteader struggle ensued. It escalated with squatters and cut fence lines and eventually ended with French shot through the head.

The round barn was built in 1882–83 by French's "buckaroos"—a slang term derived from the Spanish *vaqueros*. Conceived as a winter shelter for his horses, the low-slung building is a remarkable piece of frontier architecture. It consists of an inner stone cylinder surrounded by an outer wooden wall that is 100 feet in diameter. The roof is supported by a massive juniper post, with large juniper beams and joists. The reason for the round configuration was that the space between the two walls created a circle paddock and exercise area for breaking and training horses during long Oregon winters.

The Jenkins family purchased the property in 1916, cared diligently for the barn, and donated it to the Harney County Historical Society in 1969. It is now a state heritage site under the maintenance of the state parks, and Dick Jenkins operates an impressive new visitor's center nearby, with souvenirs and exhibits about the barn that sustain its colorful legend.

The barn was waist-deep in water during the flood years of the early 1980s. Copyright 1996, Don Baccus, dhogaza@pacifier.com

Barn builder Peter French was fatally shot by homesteader Ed Oliver. The assailant was acquitted by a jury, but he mysteriously disappeared shortly thereafter.

Opposite: The snow-dusted 1880s barn was part of one of the largest ranching operations in the Old West. It is now the hub of a historic Oregon vacation area. Photo by Bob Gibson, Blue Water Photography, Lincoln City, Oregon

Four-Generation Barn:
Macias-Bell Ranch, Wickenburg, Arizona

Given the uncertainties of life and the vicissitudes of farming and ranching in the Old West, who would have believed that the Macias barn, built in the late 1860s, would remain in the hands of family members for over a century and a quarter? The patriarch, Ramon Macias, homesteaded 160 acres along the fertile Hassayampa River, and today, 140 years later, his descendants still reside on some of the property. It holds the distinction of being one of the earliest buildings in this pioneer town named after Henry Wickenburg, an adventurer who discovered the Vulture Gold Mine here in 1863.

The barn survived through a tumultuous time, fifty years before statehood and on the heels of the wild gold rush that opened up the area in the early 1860s. The community of Wickenburg and the Macias Ranch weathered the gold exploration, General George Crook's Indian Wars, mine closures, desperadoes, drought, and a disastrous flood in 1890 when the Walnut Creek dam burst, killing nearly seventy people. There was also a resurgence of silver, copper, and gold mining and the growth of farming and ranching in the fertile floodplain before a new economy arose—the guest ranches that later labeled Wickenburg as the "The Dude Ranch Capital of the World."

According to Julie Macias Brooks, who owns a parcel of the original ranch, maintenance of the Macias barn was a continuing project that occupied several generations. Her great-great-grandfather Ramon improved the property, as did great-grandfather Francisco Macias and sons Manuel, Frank, Alfred, and Raymond. After Raymond's widow, Carrie, remarried, the property became known as the Macias-Bell Ranch.

Like many Arizona horse barns, this simple wooden structure started out small and was then expanded to meet the needs of the ranch. It housed horses and tack, and the connecting pens sheltered mules and cattle. Julie remembers playing in the barn as a child, in a high stack of hay piled in the center. She and her siblings took delight in climbing the haystack and also rummaging in the barrels of sweet feed kept for the horses. They would feed it to the horses, but it was not unusual for several kernels to also find their way into the mouths of the youngsters.

At one time, there were holding pens next to the barn where family and friends would congregate for the roundup and branding. "It was also a center place for everyone to eat lunch," she recalls, "delicious homemade tortillas, beans, salsa, and beef." After branding, some of the cattle were cut, and on those days the cowboys enjoyed "mountain oysters," with Julie's grandfather Manuel R. Macias emerging as the best cook.

The durable old barn remained in regular use until recent years and is now used mainly for storage. The gold rush in this town didn't last, but the resolute townspeople, with their strong values and historic properties such as the old Macias barn, have endured.

Down but not out, the sagging sheds have defied the odds. For many generations, they provided shelter for cattle and mules.

Rough-hewn rails and posts in the barnyard show evidence of decades of chewing and exposure to the Arizona weather.

Opposite: A barn too tough to die, this survivor remains standing, although the surrounding ranchland yielded to urban sprawl long ago.

The Barns of Reno:
Holcomb, Capurro Ranch, and Valley Road Barns, Reno, Nevada

Mention Reno, Nevada, to many easterners, and they associate it with gambling (or "gaming," as it's now called). Folks in the know will tell you that, over the years, the biggest gambles in the Silver State were the same ones they've always been—ranching and farming. Sure, the family farm has all but disappeared and agricultural production has undergone drastic evolution. But the wealth of enduring old barns and historic farmsteads in and around Reno gives testimony to an age when Nevada farmers and ranchers faced long odds and carved out a living (and more) from the land.

One example is the picturesque Holcomb Lane barn in Truckee Meadows, Reno, built by Grove and Sarah Holcomb around 1900. The barn was part of the Home Ranch, which Holcomb owned and operated. This is a gabled barn with "broken wings," the wings being a later addition. A hayloft extends the full length of the barn and has identical doors on each side. The loft is somewhat unique, in that it is supported by cables coming down from the rafters and anchored to a beam running the length of the loft. It is an interesting example of innovative construction methods of that era.

Another good example is the fading lady pictured at right, a circa 1870 barn built by the Lewis family, the original homesteaders. Back then, this grand old stock barn sat alongside a cattle trail that meandered down from Honey Lake into the verdant Truckee Valley, where green alfalfa fields and grazing cattle seem to go on forever. Today, the barn is on Valley Road, only a casino token's throw from downtown Reno. Over the years, the "city" has inched ever closer to its door, and this silent sentinel now stands in stark contrast to the commercialism surrounding it. One resident laments that "the old barn standing proudly on Valley Road, a modern blacktop boulevard, faces the possibility of a bulldozer to make room for yet another condominium."

Thanks to barn lovers and other preservationists, that is not likely to happen. The photo of the Valley Road barn by photographer Jack Hursh, a Reno native and third-generation Nevadan, won a major award at a Shooting the West symposium and has called attention to the building's rightful place as a protected landmark. These barns of Reno will not go quietly into that good night.

Capurro Ranch barn outside Reno is another splendid Nevada icon.

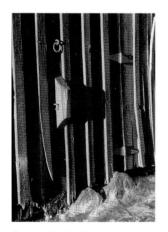

Construction detail of door to Holcomb barn.

Hursh's celebrated photo of the Lewis-Oliva barn on Valley Road may be a rallying point for preservationists who question the price of "progress."

"I Never Met a Man I Didn't Like":
Will Rogers's Barn and Stables, Pacific Palisades, California

He also could have said, "I never met a horse or a barn I didn't like." Will Rogers had a soft spot for both, and he once stated, "A man that don't love a horse … there is something wrong with him." The attention he lavished on his main barn and stables at the hilltop ranch in California was a statement to an unquenchable love for ranching, riding, and life in general.

This 1928 photo shows the overall view of "the barn" with its original taller rotunda.

Will Rogers was bigger-than-life in several dimensions … cowboy (named in the *Guinness Book of Records* for his roping feats), humorist, actor, radio personality, movie star, and social critic. Born in 1879 of Cherokee descent on an Indian Territory ranch in Oklahoma, he went on to become the star of Broadway and seventy-one movies in the 1920s and 1930s, the most popular radio personality of his time, the top-paid star in Hollywood, author of six books, besides writing more than 4,000 syndicated newspaper columns. At his prime, he was unquestionably the most popular person in America.

Will Rogers, an American original.

The immaculate stables area has nineteen horse stalls, each with its own window.

In 1928, Will and his family moved to his woodsy hilltop ranch in Pacific Palisades, a few miles west of Beverly Hills. One of his first acts was to create what he always called "the barn"—an impressive structure that housed polo ponies and riding horses. The barn was actually more assembled than built, since Will acquired two sections of horse stalls from a barn in the San Fernando Valley and directed his brother-in-law, Lee Adamson, to reassemble nineteen stalls on either side of an open-frame rotunda. (He decided the rotunda would be useful for exercising horses in bad weather.) For aesthetic reasons, he later lowered the rotunda roof closer to the level of the two wings.

In its final form, Will's beloved barn has the distinctive round canopy roof, a row of windows and open wooden louvers, and includes quarters for a stable foreman, tack room, utility room, and a wash rack. There is a big riding arena in front of the barn and a polo field nearby. The ranch became the Will Rogers State Historic Park in 1944, and it remains one of the only movie stars' estates that can be visited and enjoyed up close. The barn today serves as an equestrian center.

Opposite: Today Will Rogers's barn is part of a California historic park.

Barn Styles of the Rich and Famous:
Cabell Barn #1, Benton County, Oregon

Emily Failing and Henry Cabell liked nice things and were accustomed to getting them. Emily, the daughter of Portland politician and philanthropist Henry Failing, had recently bought out her two sisters to acquire a handsome farmstead estate in the Willamette Valley. Henry Cabell, a prominent young rancher and sportsman, purchased some desirable property directly to the south of Emily's farm.

Many Benton County folk merely attributed the two land sales to coincidence, while others dismissed them as passing extravagances of the "well-to-do." Divine providence intervened, though, when the two owners were united in marriage in 1910, the two properties were joined, and one of Oregon's most historic estates was born. In the years that followed, the Cabells not only improved the original house that was on the property—a two-story frame house built before the Civil War—but shaped an impressive farm complex that included two sizable barns, a carriage house, and a colonial-style clubhouse and lodge for visitors.

Of particular note to historians is Cabell Barn #1, a large, well-constructed barn with a gabled shake roof and a red with white trim shiplap exterior. It is notable for its refined architectural style, up-grade construction, and a more liberal use of expensive windows than is normally seen in an agricultural building. Some might say it was a little too indulgent, a little too nice for an Oregon cattle barn. On the south elevation, for example, are six-over-six double-hung sash windows and a projecting cover over a track for lifting hay into the loft. Some of the windows on the first floor have nine panes, and those on the west elevation have nine-over-nine double-hung sash. The roof has two cupolas, with louvers, and the barn rests on a deep, rock-solid concrete foundation.

Whether extravagance or investment, the barn has endured and is presently used by the Benton County Historical Society to store and display historic farm-related equipment. All the farmstead buildings are now within the Western Oregon National Wildlife Refuge complex and are registered as historic places.

The building is now serviceable as an office for a historical society.

Double-sash windows and multiple glass panes admit ample sunlight.

Opposite: This Oregon barn has an interesting configuration and more windows than most.

Great White:
Milne-Bush Barn, Northeast of Roswell, New Mexico

Just a mile or two northeast of Roswell on the old Berrendo River sits an impressive white homestead and barn—historic reminders of the Milne-Bush Cattle Company, which moved into the Pecos Valley area over a century ago. The one-room adobe homestead, built in 1884, has original vigas (one reinforced by an old wagon brace) and walls two feet thick.

The rectangular two-story barn (added around 1920) is also white and has a terneplate roof, large original beams, and an open shed area. It displays a simple linear design, with no wasted space. The roof is austere, with a moderate slope, and the second level overhangs stables and corral access on one side. Despite their apparent simplicity, the buildings are significant, because the site was the headquarters of a cattle company that was instrumental in the early settlement of southeast New Mexico.

Like all Wild West stories, this one has outlaws, too. They came along earlier, back in the 1870s. There was a small Hispanic settlement here, but a band of about twenty desperadoes shot up the place, robbed the settlement, and forced the settlers to leave the county. A few years later, the Milne and Bush Company moved cattle from other states into the Pecos range and established headquarters here.

Ranching operations were scaled down in the 1890s, however, and the last great roundup of 1894 collected 11,000 head of cattle. It continued to decline, and the property was bought by Ed Nicholas in the late 1920s and used as a hunting lodge until his death in 1949. It is a residence now and registered as a historic property.

Natural original vigas (beams) are architecturally significant.

Lodge poles provide roof support for overhanging access to the corral.

Opposite: Historic Milne-Bush barn, more than eighty years old, remains in prime condition.

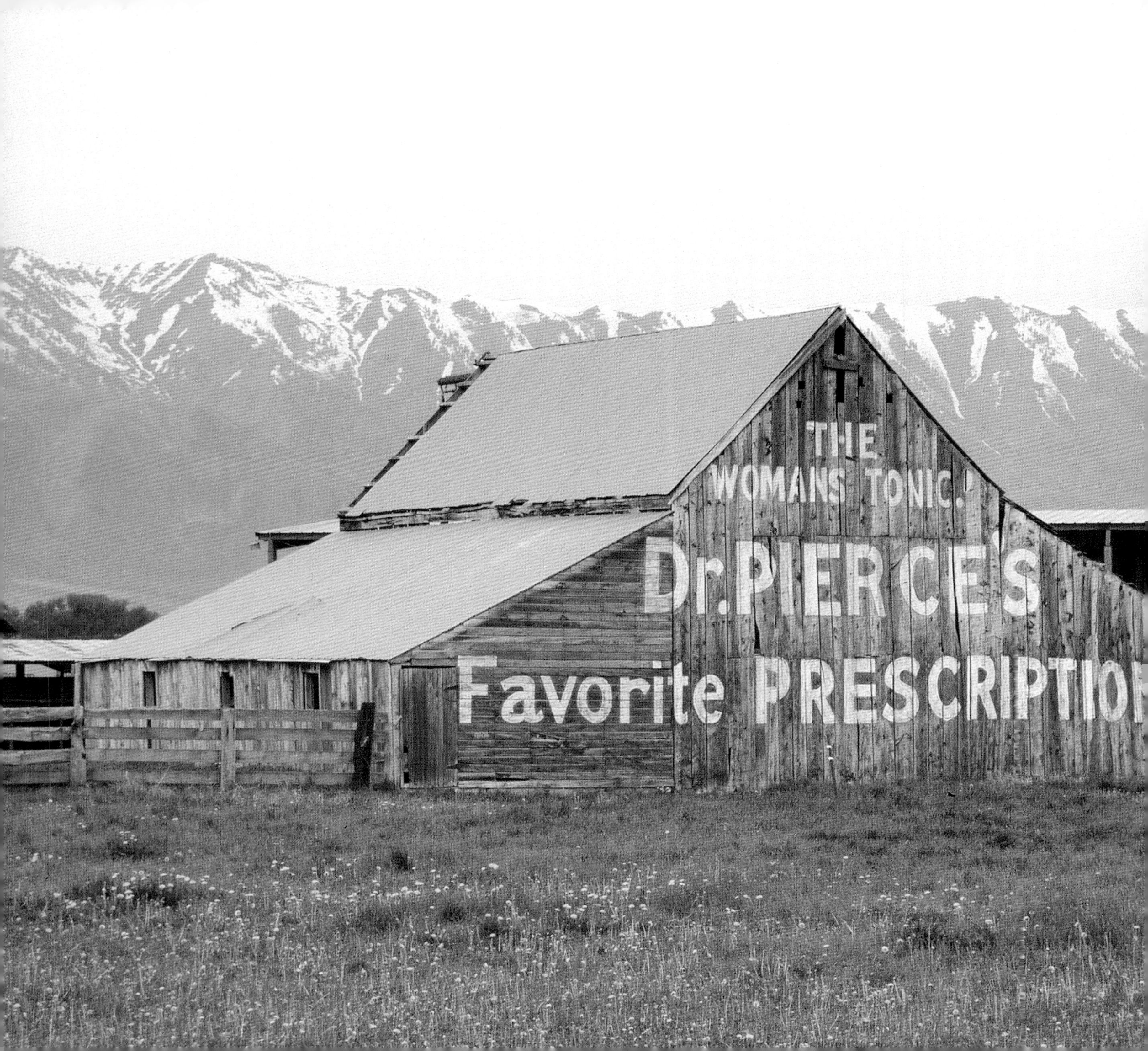
THE
WOMANS TONIC.
Dr. PIERCE'S
Favorite PRESCRIPTIO

"Dr. Pierce's Barn," Logan, Utah

Western barns have provided plenty of "wooden canvases" for painters depicting everything from elaborate murals to so-called barn ads. Whether farmers were merely marking their territory or making a statement, decorated barns have become popular landmarks, and none is more well known than the turn-of-the-century "Dr. Pierce's" signs and "Mail Pouch Tobacco" ads that first appeared during the depression.

Recent history has not been as kind to this beloved art form. Commercial barn advertising was in decline for almost three-quarters of a century before the 1965 Highway Beautification Act banned commercial advertising within 600 feet of interstate highways. Tobacco advertising in particular succumbed to the 1997 legal settlement with the tobacco companies, an agreement that forced the industry to stop outdoor advertising for tobacco products altogether.

Still, some wonderful examples of the wooden canvases remain. "Dr. Pierce's barn" in Utah's Cache Valley is one of the most photographed and appears in many books, calendars, and posters. Built in 1904 by Lovenus Olsen, the large barn was spotted by Dr. Pierce's representatives in the 1920s, and its size and highway location made it a prime high-visibility target. In exchange for $10 a year, plus a guaranteed annual sign repainting, Olsen agreed, and the ad has been there ever since. Although both the tonic and the annual barn painting have gone by the boards, the barn has not been forgotten. The lettering was freshened several years ago, and the barn itself was saved from collapse by local farmers in 1997–98. Today, the building and sign remain as familiar landmarks in this part of Utah.

This aging barn near Castle Rock, Washington, is painted on three sides with slogans extolling Dr. Pierce's products.

The "Larro Feeds" logo adorns an old barn at Bartlett Ranch, Reno, Nevada.

Opposite: "Dr. Pierce's barn," built in 1904, is located in College Ward, just south of Logan, Utah. It is one of many turn-of-the-century barns that advertised Dr. Pierce's tonics.

Legendary Round Barn:
Ojo Caliente, New Mexico

This New Mexico barn is the stuff of which legends are made. It is situated in Taos County next to a centuries-old bubbling mineral hot springs, named Ojo Caliente by the Spanish explorer Cabeza de Vaca in 1535. Ojo Caliente—"the hot eye"—referred to the eye of the five hot springs, and the therapeutic waters were a sacred spot for the ancestors of the present-day Puma Indians who inhabited the area.

Not surprisingly, a hotel and resort rose up around the legendary spa, and in 1924, a dairy barn was constructed to supply dairy products to the hotel dining room. Resembling the round Shaker barns of the 1800s and one of the few round barns in the West, it is thought to be the only one built of mud-plastered adobe bricks.

It is approximately sixty-five feet in diameter, with a ten-foot-high adobe wall topped with a thirty-foot-high round, shingled gambrel roof. At the peak of the roof is an open cupola, which ventilates the barn. The first level of the building is divided into two fourteen-foot-wide rings around a hexagonal central space. The outer ring is divided into stalls and feeding troughs, and the inner ring is primarily for farmworkers feeding the animals hay, which is dropped from the upper level into the center bin. In its heyday, the barn also included a tool room, calving room, milking parlor, and milk cooling room.

This interesting barn has earned its place as a state and nationally registered historic property and was the setting for a segment of the *Young Guns* movie. It was in a state of arrested decay until a major restoration effort in 2003.

This prerestoration interior view provides an unusual perspective of the circular barn and central manger.

Before restoration, the structure suffered from missing shingles, a collapsed cupola, and deteriorating adobe walls.

Opposite: This historic 1924 barn was completely renovated in 2003.
Photo courtesy of Historic Preservation Division, State of New Mexico Office of Cultural Affairs

An American Icon:
Three Rivers Farm Barn, Canby, Oregon

This American icon is a work still in progress. The 1904 dairy barn at Three Rivers Farm in Oregon is also known as the Kraft-Brandes-Culbertson barn (for the principal owners of the farmstead from 1900 until 1930) and was the "poster child" for the *Barn Again!: Celebrating an American Icon* exhibit from the Smithsonian Institution Traveling Exhibition Service. The barn has even been immortalized as a classic western-style barn in a miniature sculptured collectibles series by rural-life artist Lowell Davis.

All this attention is a world away from the barn's 1904 beginnings on a 290-acre farm less than a half-mile from the confluence of the Pudding and Molalla Rivers and a mile from the point where the Molalla empties into the Willamette River—hence the "Three Rivers Farm" designation.

The land had originally been owned by John Barlow, whose father built the famous Barlow Road to Oregon City in 1846. German immigrant Jacob Kraft acquired the land in 1900 and built the barn with features that include a mortise-and-tenoned timber frame, board-and-batten siding, double-pitched roof, hooded hayfork lift, and roof ridge ventilator.

Owners see to it that the big red barn continues to be upgraded.

The building measures about forty-two feet by sixty-four feet, and the ground story contained seven very large horse stalls (oversized because they housed the big draft horses used to work the fields). The hayloft above was reached by means of a hand-hewn ladder, still in use today, that extends all the way to the ridgepole. The high gable roof has a steep pitch of forty-five degrees, and the main doors are in the gable ends.

The property passed through other hands—it was sold in 1908 to Carl Brandes, Portland's first elected county auditor, and in 1920 to W. C. Culbertson, a wealthy hotel owner who made a number of improvements. It was sold again in 1930, was later subdivided, and began a decline until it was acquired by its present owners, Dr. and Mrs. Kurt Schrader, in 1982. The Schraders have made major restorations to the house and barn and are returning the property to its original prominence. The reborn barn is presently used in raising sheep, and the farm does a thriving business in strawberries and as a pickup location for farm produce.

Sheep tenants have replaced the cattle and draft horses of earlier times.

Opposite: The famed Three Rivers Farm barn in Oregon has passed the century mark but has been reincarnated to a new life.

Out Wickenburg Way:
Simpson Barn, Wickenburg, Arizona

A striking, well-designed barn of any size is a pleasure to behold, but make it big and imposing—like the old Simpson Ranch barn in Wickenburg, Arizona—and it becomes a visual treat. The structure's even rooflines and wide "footprint" yield a strong central presence in this no-nonsense working cattle ranch environment.

Aesthetically inclined historians describe this symmetrical white prairie barn as a picture of balance, with clean architectural design, an exceptionally high gambrel roof, and equal extensions reaching out on either side. Big sliding doors on the barn's gable end open into a spacious hay storage area. Horse stables are positioned on either flank of the barn, with cattle pens and roping arena nearby.

The Simpson barn appears perfectly suited to its locale and its place in history. Built in the early 1920s by the O'Brien family, it was a multiuse barn until the property was leased out in the 1930s as the first guest ranch in the area. It is used today by the Simpsons as their working cattle ranch barn, as well as for boarding horses long term. In addition, the Simpson RV Ranch adjacent to the barn provides access to the stables and barn area for visiting RVers who have their own horses.

The big white barn is clearly more than "just another pretty face." Its pleasing appearance does not detract in any way from its ruggedness and utility. In a state whose official flower is a cactus blossom, beauty and durability are constant companions.

There's hay storage room to spare inside this huge barn.

The side view silhouette rises high into the Arizona sky.

Adjacent are cattle pens, roping arena, horse stables, and a nearby Recreational Vehicle ranch.

Opposite: A handsome barn by any standards, this white prairie outpost has appeal that transcends its age.

1878 Roswell Riddle:
Slaughter-Hill Farm, Roswell, New Mexico

In an area where adobe construction prevailed, why did settler Sam Cunningham opt for a log cabin when he built his first homestead house in 1878? Considering the fact that there were no timber-size trees in the Roswell area, the newly arrived migrant from Missouri must have hauled the wood from the westward mountains—more than seventy-five arduous miles by wagon. Getting the logs there was difficult enough, but it was only part of the task Cunningham set for himself. Once on location, each log was hand hewn. And wooden pegs are used throughout—there's not a nail on the premises.

His reasons for building this log structure will never be known, but the rest of the farm's fabled history is well documented. Cunningham sold the farm in 1898 to Colonel C. C. Slaughter, a Texas "cattle king" and at one time the largest single taxpayer in the Lone Star State. Slaughter, who also purchased several adjacent Roswell farms, coveted the additional acreage to raise alfalfa for his cattle herds in Texas. Slaughter's son, George, managed the farm and brought the first registered purebred Herefords to the state of New Mexico. When Colonel Slaughter died, George gave his share of the farm to his sister, Mrs. Curtis Hill, and the property became known as the Slaughter-Hill Farm.

This simple building remains unique for its hand-hewn logs, wooden pegs, dovetailed construction, and board-and-batten eaves. It is in good condition today and is part of a stable complex where horses are raised and trained. The property is on the New Mexico and National Register of Historic Places.

Hand-hewn logs and dovetail construction are classic.

Sam Cunningham built this one to last a hundred years or more, and it has. He employed wooden pegs throughout.

Opposite: The one and a half story log building, with loft, is historically and architecturally significant and was constructed with logs hauled from more than seventy-five miles away.

Ghost Town Barn:
The Old Red Barn, Bodie, California

"Goodbye, God, I'm going to Bodie." So reads the 1880 diary of one little girl whose family was taking her to the remote and infamous hell town on the high-desert eastern slopes of the Sierra, located about fifty miles south of Lake Tahoe. The phrase became known throughout the West, and it was an apt description of the lawless town at that time.

Bodie's reputation was well deserved as having the "most wicked people and the most wicked weather" in the West. Gold was discovered there in 1859, and by 1879, the mining town supported a population of 10,000 and had taken an estimated $100 million in gold out of the ground.

It also supported more than sixty-five saloons and an incredible amount of gambling, robberies, shootings, and general hell raising. The Reverend F. M. Warrington saw it in 1881 as "a sea of sin, lashed by the tempest of lust and passion." The weather was hellish, too, with scorching summers, winters with temperatures forty degrees below zero, and winds up to 100 miles per hour whipping sand, snow, and tumbleweeds.

The boomtown lasted only a few years then faded into a ghost town, the largest one in the western United States and certainly the most well preserved. It is now a California state park, tended by the park service since 1962 in what is called a state of "arrested decay."

Among the 150 buildings remaining is a circa 1875 red barn, just one of many barns that once stood in Bodie when hundreds of horses and mules serviced the community. The modified saltbox design, with its longer side facing the prevailing winds of winter, features wood frame construction and vertical cladding. The barn was centrally located and must have been a popular spot during the town's heyday, since supplies were hauled in by horse or mule and whiskey was brought in by horse carriage, 100 barrels at a time.

Although virtually untouched for almost a century, the solitary barn shows no signs of yielding to "the West's most wicked weather" and remains a popular attraction for park visitors.

Tumbleweeds and fallen fences are reminders of the high-desert town that time forgot.

A late spring snow pile defiantly bars the doors of the 1875 barn. The old building braves scorching heat and wind in the summer, snow and ice in the winter.

The main street, silent and abandoned for more than a hundred years, with the ageless Sierras in the distance.

Opposite: A lively and long-standing "ghost" in the Bodie ghost town, the red barn was an important part of the community's thriving horse and mule commerce from the 1860s through the 1880s.

25

Chasing a Dream Westward:
James Gleed Barn, Naches, Washington

It's one thing to chase a dream from one coast to the other. It's quite another when that dream leads you through privation, loss of your family belongings, sickness, and constant concern for your own safety.

An ordinary man might have given up, but James Gleed was no ordinary man. The Massachusetts native had moved with his family from the East to Illinois in pursuit of a life as a rancher/farmer and then settled in Pueblo, Colorado. In 1878, the thirty-three-year-old farmer decided to leave Pueblo because of his poor health. With his twenty-two-year-old wife, Sarah, their four daughters, and his wife's father, Gleed packed the family's goods into a covered wagon and set out for Walla Walla in Washington Territory.

The trip was arduous and the wagon was sadly overloaded, so most of the family's home furnishings had been left by the side of the road before the Gleeds reached their destination. The dream was not to be found there, either. The community was in the midst of a diphtheria epidemic, so they continued on to the Yakima Valley.

There, after almost four months on the trail, the Gleeds could finally settle in. They could, but they didn't, because even this respite was not the homestead that Gleed had envisioned. So James Gleed took his family yet another ten miles farther up the Yakima and Naches Rivers until he found the perfect site for his 160-acre homestead (a land claim based on his forty-seven-month service in the Civil War).

With his roots planted, Gleed built a two-story frame Victorian "dream house" and in 1885 constructed a large cattle and horse barn. The heavy timber frame structure, which was built of hand-hewn posts and beams with mortise-and-tenon joints and wooden pegs, is an excellent example of the building techniques and craftsmanship of the frontier era. It is a rectangular barn, sixty-six feet by forty-four feet, and remains well preserved today. James Gleed succeeded in attaining his dream and building a good life alongside the Naches River. Through his barn, he left a little of that dream to share with us as well.

This pioneer created his own irrigation system and a six-mile canal, as well as this silo of crib construction.

The barn's "birth certificate" is proudly displayed on the wall.

Opposite: James Gleed's barn on Washington's Naches River, erected in 1885, was the end of the rainbow after an arduous journey by wagon.

Witnessing History at the O.K. Corral:
O.K. Corral Stables, Tombstone, Arizona

"I don't want any trouble, boys. Let me have your weapons." Reportedly, these futile words from Sheriff Johnny Behan were uttered shortly before the West's most famous gunfight occurred in Tombstone on October 26, 1881.

Behan was unable to prevent the confrontation between the cowboys (Tom and Frank McLaury, and Billy and Ike Clanton) versus U.S. Marshal Wyatt Earp, his two brothers, and Doc Holliday, a notorious gunfighter. When the smoke cleared, three of the cowboys were dead and two of the Earp brothers were seriously wounded. To this day, there are differing versions of exactly what happened, but there is no doubt that the legend of the gunfight at the O.K. Corral is firmly embedded in western history.

Opening onto the O.K. Corral, but far less renowned, is a barn of sorts—the adobe O.K. Corral Stables. If, as some lexicographers say, a barn is "any covered building primarily used for sheltering animals and/or storage of feed," then the covered stables will suffice as the barn closest to the famous gunfight.

Built in 1879 of sun-dried adobe blocks, the corral stables were a familiar part of old Tombstone, Arizona, and a popular place to leave (or rent) a horse or buggy. Eight men lived on the grounds, and an adjacent two-story main office contained sleeping quarters for stage drivers on the second floor. (The sixty-five-mile stage trip to Tucson took about ten hours and cost around $5.) Ritter's Funeral Parlor was located nearby, and "the town too tough to die" provided ample business—so much so that Ritter's advertisements noted that dead bodies could be dropped off at the O.K. Corral at night when the funeral parlor was closed.

The shooting lasted less than a minute on that fateful 1881 afternoon, and the acrid gun smoke dissipated quickly in the open air. But the telling of the story goes on and on. The next time you hear it, remember the fearless gunfighters who faced each other down, and remember the historic architecture that was a backdrop to the shoot-out. The O.K. Corral is now owned by the Love Family and is operated as a historical attraction.

The West's most famous gunfight is reenacted daily for visitors.

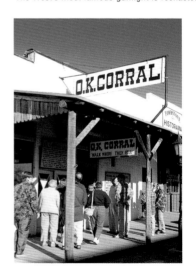
Signs invite curious tourists to "walk where they fell."

Wagons, buggies, and harnesses on display in the stable next to the blacksmith shop.

Opposite: The covered adobe-block stables at the O.K. Corral in Tombstone, "the town too tough to die."

29

Surrounded Survivor:

Cook Barn, San Juan Capistrano, California

Many historic barns sit alone, languishing in landscapes long abandoned for active farming. Either by choice or economic circumstance, neighbors have shrunk away and left them to their solitude. These are the structures that are truly "forgotten, but not gone." They remain, detached from the public, to weather winters and summers unnoticed.

For some, though, the opposite is true. One such California survivor, the Cook barn in San Juan Capistrano, has withstood an opposing force—the influx of neighbors. This windowless 1894 barn sits on a busy corner, oblivious to thousands of cars that whiz by every day on the streets that define its boundaries. It is now surrounded by a city of 30,000 inhabitants, and the cornfields and orchards that formerly flanked the structure have given way to schools, homes, and a shopping center.

The barn and the land it sits on are all that remains of a large farm established by the pioneer Cook family back in 1870. James R. Cook came west from Nebraska in 1867 by way of a wagon and ox team. His son, Rudolph B. Cook, built the barn around 1894 in a style similar to those of his native Nebraska, with stables and storage. It is built on a brick foundation and constructed of redwood from Northern California. The boards are twelve inches wide and one and a quarter inches thick. It has an earthen floor, a loft, and is topped by a cupola. Two big doors are positioned on either side of the gabled end, and the overall architectural style is one that was typical of this period.

The barn still belongs to the Cook family and presently houses farming equipment. Situated only a mile or so from the famous Mission San Juan Capistrano, it is one of the few remaining barns in this Orange County section of Southern California.

Encroaching modern-day neighbors are clearly evident and have encircled the old barn.

The walls tell their own story of changing times. Though weathering the elements well for a century, the barn has been heavily painted in recent years, more for show than to protect the durable redwood.

Opposite: The hostage California barn has weathered more than 100 years of rural-to-urban change.

Sutton's Barn Goes to College:
Sutton Barn at Eastern Washington University, Cheney, Washington

What has higher education come to? A recognition of the historical value of classic barns, that's what. And the Sutton barn on the campus of Eastern Washington University may have a better claim to being there than some of the students.

Consider the facts: The barn is nationally registered as a significant representative of "structural methods and craftsmanship" from an important era of agricultural development of the inland Pacific Northwest. No less than a respected state senator, William J. Sutton, was a one-time owner of the barn. And if you think the barn lacks the good breeding to be part of the university scene, think again. The Sutton barn was recognized as a local showplace and has served as the scene of many dignified social events. Finally, unlike some students, the old barn is paying its own way, today as offices for student services and the campus police department!

The barn has been renovated into a busy college office building.

We shouldn't be surprised. This 1884 landmark was built by William Bigham, a recognized master craftsman who didn't shy away from painstaking hand methods. It was created at a cost substantially higher than most barns and is a large braced-frame construction on a split fieldstone foundation, more than ninety feet in length and forty feet in height. Many of the rough-sawn planks exceed twenty feet in length, and the battens are milled on both edges. An unusual feature is the mortise-and-tenon braced-frame structural system, with diagonal members let into the

An old archive photo of the building before cleanup and refurbishing.

posts on shoulders and nailed, whereas the horizontal timbers are mortised and pegged with hardwood dowels.

It has certainly earned its revered place on the campus and will hopefully impart an appreciation of historical values to the students.

Opposite: The Bigham-Sutton barn (and campus offices) conceals its age of more than 120 years.

The Beat of a Different Drummer:
Max Steinke Barn, Saint John, Washington

Nobody had to tell Max Steinke that this was strange. Maybe a little foolhardy. His wife, Ida, had her doubts. Even his father cautioned against it. But at this moment in 1915, even if someone had tried to talk him out of it, Max would have turned a deaf ear. His mind was set on building a very special barn right here on Cottonwood Creek in Washington state—a round barn like the ones he had seen in his native Minnesota. Never mind that his neighbors all had traditional rectangular barns or that he already had a rectangular barn of his own on the property.

What mattered was that Max tightly clutched a drawing of a round barn design that an unknown draftsman had sketched to his exact wishes. The barn was actually not round, but dodecagonal (twelve-sided). It appealed to Steinke because of the convenience of the central feeding area and the spacious stalls for harnessing draft horses. He hired a carpenter and enlisted his younger brother, Walter Steinke, to help build this "excellent round thing." But, before starting, he tore down the old rectangular barn so that he could use its lumber for roof sheeting on the new structure. Maybe it was also a statement that there was no turning back.

A year later, and at a total cost of $1,700, the barn was completed … and it turned out to be a perfect complement to the 345-acre wheat and barley farm. With its dome roof towering sixty feet high and nine-foot-high reinforced concrete walls, it quickly became a local attraction. Twelve stalls were designed for several milk cows and the draft horses he kept for plowing, harrowing, and harvesting. Feed bins faced outward from the central hub. The trendsetting barn became the prototype of other round barns in Washington, and it has been serviceable for almost ninety years. The times have changed, but the Steinke barn remains structurally much the same as in 1916, although its roof is tattered and missing shingles. Gone are the draft horses, replaced by tractors in 1935, and the barn was later altered to better accommodate beef cattle that replaced the horses. Today it is used in this fully operational wheat ranch for feed storage for cattle. It is on the National Register of Historic Places as a "structural masterpiece" that has outlasted nearly all other barns like it, serving as "one of the outstanding structural landmarks on the landscape of the Palouse." Max would have liked that.

Pockmarked but proud, this structure led the way.

Bursts of sunlight denote missing shingles in the roof.

Opposite: The twelve-sided domed tower marks this barn architecture as truly unique.

Chisum's Jingle Bob Silvertop:
South Spring Ranch, Roswell, New Mexico

It wasn't always like this.

This quiet tree-shaded site was once the pumping heart and soul of one of the busiest cattle operations in history. In 1867, John S. Chisum blazed the historic Chisum Trail, taking a herd that originated in the little town of Paris, Texas, across the desert and north to Fort Sumner, New Mexico. For ten years, from 1874 until 1884, the famed "Pecos Valley Cattle King" made this South Spring ranch near present-day Roswell his headquarters. His estimated 80,000 head of cattle grazed a 100-mile stretch of public domain from the southeastern corner of New Mexico to Fort Sumner, and his "jingle bob" brand was the most famous in the West. It was a slit on the cow's ear, with one part standing upright and two-thirds of it bobbing.

After Chisum's death, the South Spring property was acquired by James John Hagerman, and this shiplap barn was built around 1901–02. It has large wood swinging doors, a brick chimney, and a cupola that sits atop a reflective metal roof, which has a silver or white appearance under the Roswell afternoon sun.

The historic property is now owned by Fred Visser. The barn is in excellent condition and at various times has been adapted to more civil uses, such as a museum and social hall. If John Chisum were alive, he would certainly approve. When he lived here in the Long House, he built a separate room on the back of the house for his cowpunchers to hold their dances—so "they don't beat up my Axminster carpets with their boots."

A bar is only one of the latter-day amenities in the old barn.

John Chisum, nineteenth-century cattle king, called South Spring home.

Expert shiplap construction and vertical doors.

Opposite: The "silver roof" barn in Roswell sits on a historic spot.

37

Shades of Difference:
Eclectic Idaho Barns

There are signs of evolution and modification in many western barns, but those encountered in Idaho are of particular interest. The old western ethic says to do what works, not what your neighbor does, and conformity to established architectural standards was not a priority. Agricultural buildings were no different from other buildings of the era, and the terrain, weather influences, and practical utilitarian needs shaped the structures. Many barns began as one thing and were later expanded as the needs changed.

The images shown here are similar but different—all are of early barns of wooden construction but each conceived from a different set of plans or ideas within the owner's mind. And probably all built with some sense of urgency. In Idaho, as elsewhere, barns were so essential that many early farmers built one before they built a house. But while the barns often reflected the farmer's prosperity or standing in the community, appearances seemed to matter less in the newly settled Northwest than they did in the Midwest or East.

Barn design does not always fit a stereotype of the multipurpose early barn, which housed animals on the ground floor and hay in the space above, with a large central threshing floor and the ground level divided into so many aisles or bays. Changes materialized as farming changed, and multipurpose barns gave way to more specialized barns. Farmers who raise one kind of crop, rather than the old-time mix that supported one family, conceived new barn types or adapted their existing structures. They reflect many existing architectural styles, but also hint at revisions made for unknown reasons.

Regardless of the underlying motivation, Idaho farms and ranches have left an interesting legacy for barn lovers to ponder.

Storm clouds hover over this old barn on the road to Crouch and near the Payette River. Its "broken gambrel" roof with one longer side is an interesting variation.

This interesting "half barn" overlooks pristine pastureland near Caldwell, Idaho. The reasons for its interrupted design are unknown.

Tangled ivy and green moss camouflage this reclusive old barn in Moscow, Idaho.

Opposite: This 1908 barn in Emmett, Idaho, known as the Kester barn, is silhouetted with the snowy Emmett Bench in the background. Although Spartan in style, it sports an unexpected matching cupola.

The Homecoming:
Ehart Log Barn, Weed, New Mexico

Looking at this weathered old barn, you wouldn't guess that it had touched the lives of several families—and continues to do so today. Of course, you weren't there in 1904 when settler John Ehart built the barn with his bare hands and a burning determination. He built it to survive all kinds of weather and to be the cornerstone of the Ehart Ranch, a ranch that he and his wife, Theodocia, would pass on to their offspring and heirs.

Rough hand-hewn logs have lasted a hundred years.

But John's dream died with him, because an unscrupulous son managed to wrest the ranch property away shortly before John's death and gained sole possession when Theodocia passed on shortly thereafter. The other children, who remained in the area, had no share of the Ehart property and only fading memories of the founder's vision. It remained elusive, almost forgotten, until many years later, when John and Theodocia's grandson, Jim Goss, purchased the property—unaware of its family history. It was a cousin who revealed the history to him, told how it had been sold and resold several times, and revealed that it had now propitiously come full-circle into his possession, one of the original and rightful heirs. Jim jubilantly celebrated gaining the title back, reestablished the spread, and reunited the family there.

The barn still keeps saddles and tack safe from the weather.

Today, the old hand-hewn barn remains as the symbolic hub of the extended Ehart and Goss family ranch, with farm buildings and new homes added on the property and two of John Ehart's great-granddaughters living there and doing "cow work," as Frances Goss, Jim's wife, puts it. The barn still stands, and the horses still feed in the corral next to the barn.

It is much more than a relic log house to this family. It is the symbol of a dream that was interrupted but sustained through faith and a prophetic twist or two. And when the local church convenes on Sunday morning—in the Goss living room, as it does each week—they can reflect upon the scripture, "In whom also we have obtained an inheritance, being predestinated according to the purpose of him who worketh all things."

Opposite: The double-crib Ehart barn, focal point of this family farm.

Long Barn in Apple Country:

Concrete Barn, Julian, California

Mention "barn" to most folks, and the image that springs to mind is something wooden and red. With this barn in California apple country, neither is true. This long gray-brown barn is made of sterner stuff—like concrete. Built in 1908 by architect and owner Rex B. Clark, the two-level barn is of concrete and stone construction with timber framing and measures 45 feet by more than 240 feet in length—probably the longest historic barn in the West. (For comparison's sake, it is more than twice as long as the Cooper barn, "the biggest barn in Kansas," which logs out at 114 feet.)

Originally intended as a general-purpose barn to support the owner's freight business, it housed the teams, wagons, supplies, and freight that Clark hauled from this mountain community to San Diego, sixty miles to the southwest. But it was much more than a freight terminal. The barn includes ten boxed stalls and twenty-four open stalls for horses, mules, and sheep, as well as sheep pens, a tin-lined seed bin, woodshop, kitchen, and farm manager residence. Near the barn is a blacksmith shop and outside firebox, and a wine vat and wine storage area was also on site at one time. (This area is also noted for its wines.)

The barn is now undergoing renovation by its present owners, Bob and Linda Hemborg, and will be fully restored as part of an upgraded Angus cattle and horse ranch. It owns practical values beyond its historic credentials: the unique concrete and stone construction maintains a fairly constant temperature on the lower floor of sixty-two to sixty-four degrees, and the working layout incorporates labor-saving features such as hay chutes and a grain chute to deliver feed to the livestock.

The Hemborgs' concrete barn is noteworthy, but it is not an oddity. Stone and brick unevenly found their way into American barns in the 1800s and were mostly confined to places where the necessary materials were in greater supply (limestone barns in the Shenandoah Valley, brick barns in south-central Pennsylvania, and sun-dried adobe in the Southwest). For barn lovers, this cement-sided California mountain barn adds a new and interesting dimension to western rural architecture.

The concrete building joins to the 100-year-old gate of an original homestead.

This rustic view of a barn wall appears more European than Californian.

A cavernous second level—four-fifths the length of a football field—has big hay and grain chutes to feed livestock below.

Opposite: This concrete 1908 barn, more than 240 feet in length, is nestled in a green valley near Julian, California, an old mining town that is now a haven for apple orchards.

"Born Again" Barn:
Preston Barn, Douglas County, Washington

It was the best of times, it was the worst of times. —Charles Dickens

This is the story of a 1916 barn that might have been lost except for the heroic efforts of Ed and Sheila Preston, a family who tell the story because they realized that their experience "is common to nearly every farming family who settled this region." The region is the ranching country of Douglas County, located on the high, arid plains east of the Cascades and 150 miles from Seattle. The family barn, house, and outbuildings were built with high hopes by Ed's grandparents, Hantsford and Exer Preston, in the best of times ... a "boom" period produced by twenty years of above average rainfall, a high snowpack (for summer irrigation), and favorable growing conditions. The early homesteaders had no way of knowing that the benign weather of this period was abnormal and that climatic conditions were about to revert to more typical patterns.

The harsh realities of life on the parched plains returned soon thereafter, and the "worst of times" began. Twenty years of drought followed—from the end of World War I until almost World War II—and, coupled with poor dryland farming techniques, devastated the area's economy. Many farmers were unable to survive the hard times, but the elder Prestons hung on. Over the years that followed, the old barn continued to deteriorate. When Ed and Sheila purchased the farm and were finally able to devote money to preservation, eighty years of neglect had taken its toll.

Undeterred, in 1996 they set about the three-year task of restoring the building to its original splendor, adding a new roof, rolling doors, windows, an entire new loft floor, and a new coat of paint. Today, it again stands proud. Measuring forty by seventy by thirty-eight feet high at the peak, it sits on a concrete foundation and is equipped with sixteen of the original twenty-eight plank-floored horse stalls. As Ed has written, "Preserving past identities, structures, and their history will never be easier than it is today."

Because they seized the day, the barn has been born again, and its story is an inspiration for owners faced with preservation decisions.

Before rehabilitation, the eighty-year-old barn showed years of neglect.

Using a front-end loader as a painting platform, the Preston clan refinished the aging exterior.

The completion of the "born again" barn is a lesson in stewardship for the next generation.

Opposite: The 1916 Preston Farms barn was featured in the *Barn Journal* as it underwent transformation from relic to restored landmark.

A Boy, a Barn, and a University:
Stanford Red Barn, Palo Alto, California

Stanford University stands as one of America's most renowned castles of learning, respected worldwide for its academic excellence, awards, and distinguished alumni. But if you trace its history back to the source, like a mighty river, Stanford starts with a visionary man, lazily winds around past an old barn, and eventually runs through the heart of a fifteen-year-old boy. Stanford's story includes all of these, as well as the apparition of the Palo Alto Stock Farm existing today in one of its still-standing original nineteenth-century barns.

One might have thought that the words "nothing succeeds like success" were spoken precisely of Leland Stanford. In California in 1884, Stanford was on top of the world. He had served nobly as governor (and was later to represent the state in the U.S. Senate) and was both respected and reviled as a wealthy railroad tycoon. Eight years earlier, he had hammered the golden spike at Promontory, Utah, that created a transcontinental railroad and hastened our nation's westward expansion.

An innovative administrator but no office-bound, one-dimensional figure, Stanford also developed a famous 8,000-acre stock farm for trotting horses down on the ranch in Palo Alto ("tall tree" in Spanish). At its height, the farm employed 150 workers and boarded 600 horses. It was here that Stanford, using his own theory of bloodlines, developed trotters that set nineteen world records. But raising horses was much more than a hobby indulged in by a wealthy man. In the years preceding the development of the automobile, Stanford reasoned that careful breeding of horses could increase their productivity, thereby boosting the U.S. economy. (There were approximately 13 million horses in the country in the late 1800s.) The Red Barn, built in 1878, was an important part of the stock farm and of Stanford's life.

But as much as he loved his Palo Alto Stock Farm and his wife, Jane, the light of his life was his only son Leland Jr. Young Leland, like his father, loved the life on the ranch. He kept dogs and horses, knew all about farm machinery, and built a miniature railroad on the grounds with 400 feet of track. Although he was a studious young man, fifteen-year-old Leland Jr. spent much of his time "cowboying" around the barns.

Tragically, while away with his family on a trip to Italy in early 1884, young Leland contracted typhoid fever, and his promising life came to an end two months before his sixteenth birthday. When the boy died, his father tearfully announced to his wife, "The children of California shall be our children." Those words were the beginning of Stanford University, as the Stanfords donated their millions in remembrance of their young son, turning the celebrated Palo Alto Stock Farm into the site of the university.

Today, the Red Barn is home to the Stanford Equestrian Center, located on thirteen acres of the campus that was part of the original horse breeding farm and one of the few remnants of the scientific breeding and horse training that took place here between 1876 and 1903. The barn was painstakingly and lovingly restored in 1984.

Inside the Red Barn today. It remains an active horse facility.

The big red barn and adjacent stables provide an equestrian center for horse management instruction and group and individual riding lessons.

Opposite: The expansive Stanford Red Barn, now home to the Stanford Equestrian Center, was completely restored in 1984.

The Self-Sufficient Farmstead:
Schatz Farm, Clackamas County, Oregon

Every now and then, a person, place, or thing comes along that perfectly suits its dictionary definition. Up in northern Oregon, in Clackamas County, is the epitome of a farmstead: "the buildings and adjacent service areas of a farm." The all-inclusive Robbins-Melcher-Schatz farmstead of the late 1800s not only included the obligatory farmhouse (circa 1860) and a respectable barn, but also had a machine shed, milk house, nut house, ham house, smoke house, brooder house, chicken coops, water tower, and outhouse. There may be a few others, but who's counting?

When the independent Schatz brothers, Jake and John, built a barn in 1906 to replace an earlier smaller barn, they applied the same self-sufficient thinking to that structure. First, it had to be their own design, not someone else's idea of what a barn should be. Second, it had to be "from the land"— every piece of lumber felled on the property and hand-hewn on the site. (They wouldn't hear of buying lumber when they had a decent stand of their own.) And the structure had to be big enough to take care of their needs "for quite a spell."

This is good country up here in Clackamas County. The rich, dark soil is turned over in the bottomland, furrowed as if a giant hand had been pulled across it, and the pastures are dotted with cows. Like most faithful tillers of the soil, the self-reliant Schatz boys honored their pact with the environment. They carefully selected the timber to be taken, used axes and crosscut saws to fell the trees, and then they dragged them out of the woods and began shaping the structure that they had seen in their minds. When they were through, you could tell this was a labor of love, created in and of the land.

The resulting Schatz barn, standing thirty-five feet tall, forty-eight feet wide, and seventy-eight feet long, was one of the larger barns in the area. It met the needs of the Schatz brothers and served faithfully as a general-purpose barn until 1983. Restoration began in 1984, and the barn and farmstead have now been upgraded and renovated for another century. The celebrated barn is deserving of this attention, because, as farm folks said back then, "the barn is the heart of the homestead."

The interior may get a little messy after a hundred years, but the building is being tidied up now for another century.

The water tower near the house is just another of many outbuildings.

Opposite: The Schatz barn is part of a completely self-sufficient Oregon farmstead of the late 1800s.

Feat of Clay:
Alvino Fritze Adobe Barn, La Mesilla, New Mexico

adobe: noun, 1. building material of heavy clay, earth, and straw; 2. a structure made of adobe bricks.

Alvino Fritze must have beamed with pride whenever he viewed his handsome new adobe barn on the property in La Mesilla. This large unplastered adobe, with its gabled roof and two sliding metal doors, was a fitting adjunct to the 1875 home and blacksmith shop nearby. The barn was a latecomer, built around 1915, but it was no less significant. In the ensuing years, it proved so, serving as a multiuse agricultural barn and eventually gaining notoriety as a registered historic property "important for its size and uniqueness."

The barn was built in the simplest of styles, with barn doors placed in the wide side rather than the gabled end, a throwback to old English barns. The sturdy foot-thick adobe walls were certainly native to the local culture, though, and the windowless walls gave excellent insulation against heat and resistance to erosion from moisture. In this dry climate, the Fritze barn was perfectly suited to its locale and purpose.

The barn belonged to a time and territory that was also unique in southwestern U.S. history. La Mesilla was founded by the Spanish in 1598, under Mexican rule until the Gadsden Purchase of 1854, and was the Confederate capital of the region during the Civil War (and site of wrangling and bloodshed between its residents of divided loyalties). In postwar years, its eminent visitors included Lew Wallace, who wrote the novel *Ben-Hur* while governor of New Mexico, famous Indian scout Kit Carson, and the infamous Billy the Kid, who was lodged in the La Mesilla jail.

The barn itself was witness to a splash of local color when Alvino Fritze's daughter, Josefina, married Simon Guerra. Simon was the local judge and held court in the blacksmith shop next door to the barn, using the big anvil as his "bench" and seat of justice.

Today, the barn is owned by Joni Guiterrez, who is staunchly dedicated to its preservation. It is not now in use, except as home for a pair of itinerant barn owls, but remains a steadfast symbol of the area's colorful past.

Sliding metal doors in the barn's wide side are still fully functional.

Sign of the times: adobe barns are impervious to heat and moisture in this dry area, but deteriorate if they begin to crack or lean. This one is going through a slight separation but remains structurally sound.

Long considered to be lucky, barn owls help keep insects and rodents away. The adobe barn has a pair as its present tenants.

Opposite: Situated in the middle of an area steeped with history, this unplastered adobe has stood since 1915.

51

Ranch to Farm to Historic Park:
Irvine Ranch Barn, Irvine, California

Populous Orange County, California—"the Big Orange"—is known for Disneyland, Newport Beach, the Laguna art colony, and a host of other attractions. But long before it had an airport named John Wayne and a university named Irvine, it had the spacious Irvine Ranch. Its owner was James Irvine, an Irishman who made his fortune as a San Francisco merchant during the California Gold Rush and acquired the 93,000-acre ranch by way of a Spanish land grant in 1876. When James Irvine died in 1886, his son James Irvine II took over and promoted large-scale cattle ranching there in the late 1800s.

An early photo of another of the Irvine barns.

The visionary Irvine was also responsible for boldly transforming the ranch from grazing to farming in the early 1900s and laying the foundation for a Southern California agricultural empire. Herds of cows and flocks of sheep were replaced by barley, orange groves, beans, and sugar beets. Cattle ranching was curtailed, although it continued actively for many years and to a modest extent even today.

A big red carriage barn was one of several buildings built in 1895 when ranching was at its peak, and it is still a part of the local landscape. The barn played a multipurpose role and held not only carriages, but also feed for the mules kept at the compound, served for a time as a blacksmith shop where buggies and tractors were repaired, and later housed the Irvine family cars.

A dozen or so buildings that were part of the original ranch are now being restored and refurbished as central components of a new Irvine Ranch Headquarters Regional Park, and the storied barn will serve as a museum of turn-of-the-century farm equipment.

A resurrected wagon will again be on display at the ranch.

Cowboy George Studley, shown in this 1925 photo, was one of many who worked the sprawling Irvine cattle ranch.

Visitors to the ranch buildings will even be able to stroll amid the ranch's original vegetation—including a driveway lined with palm trees, Valencia orange groves, poinsettias, and bougainvillea. The park is intended to give a glimpse of life here at the turn of the century. The old red Irvine barn is a prominent, and apparently permanent, part of it.

Opposite: This reborn California barn will sit in a new regional park.

Air-Born Barn in Arizona:
Flying E Ranch, Wickenburg, Arizona

No, that's not a misspelling. This unique barn—and the sprawling ranch that surrounds it—was literally "born" from the air. The 3,000-acre site was purchased in 1946 as a fly-in private ranch by aviator Lee Eyerly and his sons, and it grew up around their 3,200-foot airstrip. The airstrip accommodated guest planes and also served for a time as the town airport. Even the name and cattle brand is drawn from the Eyerlys' love for the air: the "Flying E," with wings on either side of the initial.

As luck would have it, the ranch was also seen from the air in 1949 by former guests George and Vi Wellik of California, who were flying in their private plane. The Welliks proceeded to buy the property in 1951, added 17,000 acres, and developed what is now the Flying E Guest Ranch, one of the premier such facilities in the West.

To the wide-eyed vacationer viewing the ranch for the first time, it's almost too big and beautiful to be real. With all that wide-open rangeland and rolling desert hills under sunny Arizona skies, you can understand the surreal surroundings. But it's a real guest ranch, a "riding ranch," with plenty of cattle and horses and visiting "guest hands" in the middle of the action.

The distinctive round-roof barn is certainly for real, and it houses shops, a tack room, and all the riding accessories and activities—not to mention an occasional square dance in a beautiful cedar hayloft. The barn was built in 1946, a Johnny-come-lately among historic structures, but a new breed of ranch building destined to make its own history.

The clean log construction of this distinctive barn complements its classic architectural lines.

The insistent ranch bell keeps things on schedule.

Good advice for budding cowboys.

Opposite: The arched-roof barn provides an imposing backdrop for riders mounting up.

State of the Art:

T. A. Leonard Round Barn, Pullman, Washington

If you are inclined to like round barns, then you will certainly be taken by Thomas Andrew Leonard's twelve-sided structure built in Washington state in 1917. Even died-in-the-wool aficionados of "traditional" rectangular barns admit that the Leonard barn is a superb effort and respect its revered status as one of the few round barns remaining in the state. Not that round barns need any defending. George Washington designed and built one of the first recorded ones in North America in 1796, a sixteen-sided polygonal barn on his farm in Fairfax County, Virginia, and even that historic landmark was eclipsed by the famous 1826 Shaker round barn near Hanover, Massachusetts.

But round barns remained somewhat of an oddity until the latter part of the nineteenth century. Then farmers began a historic shift from self-sufficiency to production for market, and the round barn was heralded by its proponents as being more efficient and convenient than traditional styles. They had a strong argument. It enclosed more square feet per lineal length of wall, required 30 to 50 percent less material, and was better lighted and ventilated.

All this was not lost on Thomas Leonard. An astute farmer, teacher, and homesteader, Leonard had migrated from Pennsylvania to Washington's Palouse region a few years earlier. When a fire destroyed his own rectangular barn, Leonard moved expeditiously to build a more productive and efficient barn. He researched farm periodicals for plans and consulted with Max Steinke, another Washington farmer who had built a round barn a year earlier. Leonard, however, raised the design to new levels, with stud wall construction rather than concrete walls to allow more windows for light.

What emerged in 1917 from the ashes of his old barn was a near-perfect new round structure, measuring fifty-eight feet in diameter and more than forty-five feet in height, sheathed with shiplap siding, and topped by a bell-shaped roof covered with cedar shingles. When the atypical barn was finished, Leonard indulged another uncharacteristic liberty and painted it green and white. It remains a local landmark and a prime example of this barn style.

Like an emerging bud, the Leonard barn rises above its neighboring farm buildings.

A "manure trolley" travels around the entire perimeter on a metal rail and is used for collecting manure and exiting to the outside for disposal.

Opposite: Precise in detail, the multistory structure is better lighted than most round barns of its era.

The Big Red One:
Dogie Jones Ranch, Watrous, New Mexico

What's the life expectancy of a wood-construction hay barn? Forty years? Sixty years? The proud elder shown here is more than ninety years of age and going strong.

This primary landmark on the picturesque Dogie Jones Ranch in Mora County, northeastern New Mexico, has aged well. It is one of four very large hay barns of wood construction, with vertical side boarding and corrugated metal gambrel roofs, that were built in 1913. They were erected by William Kronig Jr., son of one of the most respected pioneers in the area and grandfather to its present owner, G. M. "Dogie" Jones. Kronig's heirs have treated this particular property with respect, and they have had some luck, too.

Life is not easy for a hay barn. Two of the four Kronig-built barns are gone, lost to lightning. Even Big Red has fended off its share of electrical storms, but Jones says its biggest threat was man-made. A transient slept overnight in the barn and built a small fire. "He covered it up the next morning before he moved on," related Dogie, "but those cow chips can smolder for hours." It eventually triggered a blaze, but local firefighters came to the rescue and contained the damage.

From the start, the barn has been used as it was intended, for feed storage for the large cattle ranch, rather than housing animals. There is no loft, and in the old days, the barn would be stuffed from floor to roof with loose hay. With today's baled hay, though, a barn this size could hold enough feed for several counties.

The barn, from porch to porch, measures 65 by 140 feet, and the height is 37 feet to the pitch. There are three vents on top, each about four feet high. It sports a sound architectural design, with a continuous broad overhang supported by tree trunk posts at the eves of the gambrel roof. In the center of both flanks of the barn is a gabled roof wagon entrance, which facilitated unloading of hay wagons. The nationally registered historic site continues in full use today and is a dominant landmark on the local horizon.

The barn bears the "Walking O" brand. Its owner is a respected quarter horse breeder who got into the horse business after working as a state livestock inspector.

This ranch signpost beckons travelers down the road to the 1913 hay barn on the historic Santa Fe Trail. Nearby is an original stagecoach building and well-preserved wagon ruts from the famous route that connected Missouri and New Mexico from 1821 until 1880.

Opposite: A historical and architectural landmark in the Mora River Valley, this big red barn can be seen for miles.

Leaving a Trace:
The Everlasting Barns of Idaho

Nowhere is the spirit of preservation more vibrant than in Idaho. And with good reason. There are many surviving early buildings and barns that are worth saving and that are leaving a trace. With an active State Historic Preservation Office and involved groups inventorying historic sites, the preservation movement is staunchly defending the faith. It helps, of course, to have people like Boise journalist and photographer Ken Levy, who has made a point of capturing dozens of priceless barns on film. Some of these images are shown here—interesting old characters and battered-but-unbowed survivors in their natural settings.

Stone walls do not a barn make, but they serve this 1914 farm structure quite well. The rugged Idaho dairy barn overlooks Lemmon Falls.

A remaining structure of merit is the 1914 volcanic stone dairy barn situated near the edge of a basalt canyon in Wendell, Idaho. The property belonged to Minnie Miller, who owned a Guernsey dairy on the nearby island at Thousand Springs. The Nature Conservancy purchased the dairy and Miller properties from the heirs in 1986, then sold the upper house and barn to Jack and Donna Scott in the late 1990s. One of their first orders of business was to replace roofing because, as Donna says, "the rooftop was literally blowing away, shingle by shingle." They are continuing major repair of the barn and may establish a museum in the loft to celebrate the region's dairy heritage.

The snow-surrounded Homer Beal barn pictured here is located near Ola Mountain and was a 1930s model of simplicity. Beal's son, Roger, says they kept saddle and work horses on one side, milk cows and a separator on the other, with hay storage in the middle. Homer Beal chopped hay using a chopper, "and it just blew in there and we'd fork it out as we needed it," said Roger. The barn is situated at the confluence of the Soldier and Little Squaw Creeks in Ola Valley and is destined to remain there for posterity.

The Beal barn and scattered cattle stand out from their snowy setting in Idaho's Ola Valley.

These are much more than quaint rural buildings. They are moments in time that must not be allowed to slip away unnoticed. The Idaho state motto says it best: *Esto perpetuo* (It is forever).

Opposite: The Long family barn near Horseshoe Bend, Idaho, is typical of many in this area.

61

Colorado Log Barn Is a Winner:
Trevarton Ranch Barn, Estes Park, Colorado

Picture yourself 8,000 feet up in the Colorado mountains, in the shadow of Rocky Mountain National Park, surrounded by high mountain meadows dotted with tall pine trees. This idyllic site is home to Trevarton Ranch (also known as Big Elk Ranch), a fourth-generation family ranch that has recently undergone a startling rebirth. At its core is a ninety-two-year-old log barn, whose restoration won a Barn Again! Farm Heritage award from *Successful Farming* magazine and the National Trust for Historic Preservation.

The barn's owner, Gary Williams, has been linked to the Trevarton Ranch for as long as he can remember. As a boy, he spent his summers helping his grandparents, Phillip and Lillian Trevarton, with their cow-calf operation. Before that, the log barn was the center-piece of a mixed farming operation that raised turkeys and chickens, grew some hay and vegetables, and also had a dairy operation that could house and milk up to 100 cows.

When ill health forced the grandparents to move off the 2,000-acre ranch, it was leased out for several years before Williams was able to move onto the property and take over its operations. It needed full-time attention. As the land had become more valuable over the years, ranching had become less profitable. "I had offers to sell to developers," said Lillian Trevarton, "but I was always determined to keep the ranch." That opportunity arose when Boulder County purchased the development rights in a unique arrangement that preserves the land as open space but allows it to continue as a working ranch. It also provided the cash to invest in improvements starting with the 100-by-60-foot log barn.

Gary Williams made all the right moves, attending a workshop on barn preservation and lugging home plenty of ideas for fixing up the neglected barn. The roof's rotting boards and rusty tin were stripped away and a new red steel roof took its place. New cross braces were added to stabilize the sides, which had been miraculously standing on their own for years. Then Williams jacked up the sides of the barn, poured a new founda-tion, and replaced the rotted sill logs, finally restoring the weather-worn original logs with a coat of linseed oil mixed with lacquer thinner.

The old barn has been reborn. The central part is again used for hay storage, with a shop and a tack room occupying the two side bays. The renovated ranch now rents out pasture for cattle in the summer and fall and boards up to seventy head of horses during the winter and spring. Additional income is generated from several sources: 4,000 bales of hay sold to dude ranch operators, firewood sales, and leasing parts of the ranch for hunting outfitters in the fall and dude ranch operators during the summer.

The whole extended Williams family has pitched in to do chores and make the ranch a success, and the restored barn provides some of the inspiration. In the words of Lillian Trevarton, "The barn is a landmark, a centerpiece, and a great source of pride for the ranch." It is also a model for fully restoring an aging farm building to a new functional use.

Before: Years of neglect are apparent before the rescue takes place.

After: Spruced up inside and out, the award-winning barn has been restored to full ranching use.

Opposite: The revitalized Trevarton Ranch project in Colorado proves that even an aging log barn can be given new life and put to productive new uses.

The Music Man's Other Opus:
Albert Green Barn, Battle Ground, Washington

It was early October in 1901 and the seasons were changing guard, leaving summer behind and getting nature ready for an uncertain Washington fall and winter. In the little town of Lewisville, darkness was descending and the fading light along the Lewis River was changing the big trees from detailed lattices of branches and leaves into singular dark, indistinct shapes.

Here at Albert and Letha Green's house, a few straggling music students had just finished their rehearsal and were bundling up before trudging off into the night. The music master himself, Albert Green, busied himself putting away the large linen music charts that he had used for years to teach the Vocal Music School. This was just another final rehearsal before yet another community concert, a fund-raiser that was the culmination of six months of Albert's volunteer work. But Albert Green was happy with the result. Happy, too, because as everyone in Lewisville knew, Albert was passionate about his music.

Five hundred yards south of Green's house stood his other passion: a very large, very square barn whose construction reflected the same level of diligence that Albert applied to his music. The barn had been on his mind ever since he first arrived in this valley from Canada fifteen years earlier. Now that it was recently finished (you could smell the cut lumber), it was an impressive sight to behold.

The bank barn measures sixty feet by sixty feet, rising to a height of forty-five feet at the ridge of its gabled roof. At ground level, major support posts rest on uncut fieldstones, and one of the girders is a single peeled log sixty feet in length. The lowest level, with cattle stalls and feed pens, has two parallel aisles running north south. The middle level, with horse stalls, has a single central aisle reached by ramps on either side and oriented east west. Up above is a gigantic haymow with access in the north and south gabled ends.

Perhaps Albert Green felt in this impressive barn some of the same sense of structure and harmony that he lived in his music. One thing we know today: Lewisville no longer exists, and a lot of water has passed under the Lewis River bridge since that night more than a hundred years ago. But Albert Green's reputation both as a music teacher and a barn builder is intact, and so is the big square barn he built.

A single peeled log, sixty feet in length, is the main girder.

The tack room is undisturbed in the music man's masterpiece.

Opposite: The century-old Washington barn's three levels are for cattle, horses, and hay storage.

65

Coats of Many Colors:
A Who's Who of Western Barn Hues

Ask most folks to name their favorite barn colors, and their first three picks are red, dark red, and light red. Many may be surprised to learn that not all barns are painted red. They may be even more surprised to discover that many western barns are not painted at all. Western barns get a bad rap from visitors migrating from the eastern shore, folks who say the gray, weathered barns look "uncared for." That's because many are built of redwood and Douglas fir, woods that do quite nicely without paint 'n powder and are best left untreated.

In a recently published collection of barn photos, the color white ranked second to red. White barns are indeed impressive sights in the rural landscape. White paint has long appealed to owners of dairy barns to accentuate their claims of cleanliness, and it became the preferred color when some government certification programs actually required that dairy barns be whitewashed inside and out. Off-white, slate gray, tan, and earth-tone barns are also popular, and there are a number of structures painted varying tones of green and blue.

Is the color important? Probably not, except to a barn painter. There are plenty of them, of course, and a goodly number of tales and jokes about barn painting and lessons to be learned from it.

For example, one tongue-in-cheek story points out that not everyone who paints a barn can be relied upon to do a capable job. A farmer was looking to hire a painter when a retired church deacon applied. The deacon underbid others and got the assignment, but he yielded to his darker side and decided the only way to make any money on this painting job was to thin the paint liberally with turpentine.

He was high up on the barn on his ladder applying the thinned-down paint when the sky suddenly darkened and an ominous storm came up. As the thunder boomed and the rain came down, the thin, weak paint began streaming down the sides of the barn. Then a lightning bolt struck the ladder and sent the deacon tumbling to the ground.

Lying there in the pool of washed-off paint and turpentine, he looked heavenward and cried out in a conscience-stricken voice, "What must I do?" A mighty voice boomed down out of the storm clouds, "Repaint! Repaint! And thin no more!"

Red-roofed green barns lend a splash of color to a forest setting in Glenoma, Washington.

Blue-gray rural architecture near Rock Lake, Washington, is easy on the eye.

A multicolored barn in Artesia, New Mexico, appears confused over what color it wants to be.

Opposite: The color of this 1930 forest service barn in Randle, Washington, matches its woodsy environment.

History Is Alive at Sno-Shoe:
Sno-Shoe Ranch Log Barn, Glenrock, Wyoming

In the spring of 1886, four years before Wyoming became a state, an intrepid rancher with an unlikely name homesteaded and built a log cabin in the foothills of the Laramie Mountains. The homesteader, Ulysses Simpson Grant, bore the same name as the U.S. president, but none of the other advantages. More than gently "settling" into this valley, Grant hacked and gouged a ranch and a living from it in an area with rock mounds and spruce-covered mountains that are thumped with heavy snows in the winter and whose roads, even today, are often impassable from October until June. Today, defying all odds, the buildings endure, and the ranch built in the nineteenth century is still lived in by Grant's descendants in the twenty-first century.

The historic site is the Sno-Shoe Ranch, south of Glenrock, Wyoming. The property and log barn have been owned by the Grant family since they first began running cattle in the area, and the ranch is practically unchanged despite passage of more than a hundred years. The original homestead cabin is still in use, and the barn, corrals, and even a 100-year-old lodgepole snow fence still serve their original purpose.

The ranch covers 12,500 acres and has a 200-head cattle operation. Winter is often long and always harsh, and snowshoes are handy when you're feeding cattle in six feet of snow. The setting and the structures haven't changed, except for the addition of electricity, but some of the ranching methods have. The Grants have a herd of horses on the ranch, but they now use motorcycles and four-wheelers for herding, checking calves, and fence repair.

The weathered, old 1800s barn was built from lodgepole pine logs cut from the canyons nearby and was constructed with large logs on the bottom eight feet and boards above chinked with mud and strips of wood. It accommodates cattle and a dozen horses, with a hayloft above the horse barn. The barn was recognized by the National Trust for Historic Preservation in 1994 as a classic example of venerable American barn architecture remaining in practical service. In a world that increasingly measures time in milliseconds, it is reassuring that time has stood still here in the Wyoming foothills.

The 1880s log cow shed is well used today, as always, in the ranch's cow/calf operations.

It's hard to believe that this century-old barn, built from lodgepole pine logs, is still filled with hay every winter and remains an active part of an active ranch.

Opposite: The Sno-Shoe Ranch in Wyoming was homesteaded more than 100 years ago, constructed of materials all harvested on the property. It won a Barn Again! national award for its preservation and practical use.

Historic Round Barn Rescued:
Laughlin Barn, Castle Rock, Washington

What, you may ask, is significant about the oldest round barn in Washington or, for that matter, in the Pacific Northwest? Well, several things. It's incredible that an 1880s-built barn still stands at all after more than a century of major storms in the area, forest fires, several earthquakes, and a volcanic eruption.

But the oldest round barn here is important for another reason: because only a handful were built in the state of Washington, and this one was built on the leading edge of the 1880–1920 round barn heyday, long before it became politically correct to "think outside the box."

The Laughlin barn is also significant because Sam Laughlin employed some unique construction principles. Large members of the framing structure, including the massive center post, are hand hewn, split, or planed. On the ground floor are many inward-facing stalls for horses and cows, and the sixty-three-foot-diameter outer wall is supported by a ring of twenty split posts that are breast high to the loft. The most striking feature of the large upper-level loft is the fan-shaped bracing that radiates from the center post to support the rafters "like a giant umbrella."

Even with all this going for it, the structure narrowly escaped extinction in recent years. In 1995, the barn roof was lost in a strong windstorm. The owner and several members of the local community rallied to its plight and formed something called the "Cowlitz Round Barn Preservation Association," restoring the entire support structure and roof. (The roof alone cost $50,000.) The roof beams, some in excess of twenty-five feet, were custom milled by a local company with trees felled on the property—just like the originals. In fact, when the restoration effort fell behind schedule, the mill owners gathered family members who came out to finish the job as volunteers. The association rescued this treasure and is intent on maintaining it and others in the area.

These custom-milled roof beams from the property were made just like the original ones.

The Laughlin round barn is nestled in a wooded Washington valley.

Opposite: This 1880s structure has been staunchly protected by perservationists in its Washington community.

Legendary Camel Barns of Benicia:
U.S. Army Arsenal, Benicia, California

The facts are clear … as clear as thousands of yellowing pages of U.S. Army records and several historical texts can be. They show that in 1855, Jefferson Davis—pre–Civil War U.S. secretary of war and later wartime president of the Confederacy—got an idea for carrying military supplies across the western deserts and mountains that blocked our nation's expansion toward the Pacific Coast. After the Mexican-American War, much of the U.S. Army was deployed in the West, and the cost of supplying those outposts was alarming. His answer: camel caravans.

He convinced Congress to spend $30,000 to import seventy-eight camels from Tunisia, Egypt, and Turkey. The animals, and the soldiers who rode them, formed the U.S. Army's one and only Camel Corps. The soldiers spent about a year getting acquainted with and training their new steeds but soon discovered that the camels spat and bit when annoyed, resisted handling, and were generally smelly and cantankerous.

Nevertheless, they could carry much heavier loads than horses or mules, could withstand desert heat, did not stampede, and did not need as much food or water. There was even talk of the camels carrying mail or hauling artillery pieces westward to help subdue unruly Indian tribes.

Truth is, it started and ended as an experiment. There was never a substantial Camel Corps, and the army was often at a loss as to what to do with the herd. The beasts were used in several ways—mostly in support of Edward Beale's government contract to survey and develop the 35th Parallel wagon road to California. It was during that assignment that they were employed in their only "camel charge." When the civilian road workers were set upon by Mojave Indians east of the Colorado River, it was civilian packers and laborers, not soldiers, who mounted the camels, charged, and routed the Mojaves.

The camel experiment was eventually dashed, however, by the tide of history—the Civil War came along and support for the idea dissolved. The camels were transferred in 1861 from Fort Tejon to the Los Angeles Quartermaster Depot, and thirty-five of the animals were later sent to the Benicia Arsenal in Benecia, California, to be auctioned off. They were sold within a few weeks and used by civilians in commercial hauling and mining operations.

Before they were sold, the camels stayed at two native-sandstone storehouses at the arsenal, but what is not 100 percent clear is whether the thirty-five camels were actually ever stabled in the sandstone buildings or behind the buildings. Reputable historians maintain that there was a corral outside the storehouses, but one legend here has the camels inside the buildings. Regardless, the site is known only as the "Benicia Camel Barns," the historic buildings are a fixture in the local community, and a museum is now housed in the major barn. Although the camels are long gone, they are firmly enshrined in western history and have even inspired annual camel races in the city each summer.

The Clocktower Fortress, built in 1859 to protect the military post from Indian attacks, is now used for community functions.

Opposite: The sandstone Benicia Camel Barn played a part in the curious saga of the Camel Corps created by Jefferson Davis before the Civil War.

Big Sky and Beyond:
Child Kleffner Ranch, East Helena, Montana

Montana's Big Sky country, described by many as America's "last best place" to live, certainly provides some of our most picturesque farm- and ranchlands, as well as a number of historic and legendary barns.

Take the Kleffner barn, for example, looking for all the world like a structure that was fused together from volcanic rock and a stand of Montana timber. This stone-and-wood barn at the historic Child Kleffner Ranch in East Helena, Montana, was built in 1888 by William Child and is one of the largest barns of its age in the country. It has three floors, seventy windows, is fifty-four feet high at the peak, and totals more than 27,000 square feet of floor space. When William Child planned his ranch along Prickly Pear Creek, he wanted it to be "a showplace around the whole United States." At least those are the feelings of Paul Kleffner, who bought the property in 1943. "Everything he did here, he did just superbly," Kleffner said. "He just didn't skimp." Kleffner is probably right, as an official appraisal of the property described the building as "one of the oldest, largest, and most historic barns in the western United States."

When Child originally built the barn, he had developed a ranch of around 3,000 acres with a nest egg accumulated from mining ventures. Built of glacial rock by thirty Italian stonemasons, the barn was its focal point, a structure that could house 500 head of cattle and store more than 300 tons of hay. The timbers, rafters, and beams were put together with mortise-and-tenon joints held with oak pins. It was built at a unique time in Montana history, just after the severe winter of 1886–87—a disastrous event that solidified Child's belief that cattle could not roam the open range in Montana winters.

Child also built an unusual stone octagonal house, with a second floor that consisted entirely of a maple-floored ballroom large enough to accommodate 100 couples. After completing the buildings, however, Child lost the property because of his debts. One of Montana's first two U.S. senators, Wilbur Fisk Sanders, took over the property in 1893, and Child died at the ranch a month later. His death was speculated to be suicide stemming from despondency over the loss of the property. The ranch and the splendid old barn passed through a number of hands and were owned by the Federal Land Bank when Paul Kleffner acquired them in 1943. Paul and Thelma Kleffner turned the run-down ranch into a beautiful spread again, patiently restoring the buildings and creating a comfortable home for their growing family. A silent witness to over a century of Montana history, it has been on the National Register of Historic Places since 1977.

Thirty Italian craftsmen labored to create the stonework of this massive three-story barn a year before Montana achieved statehood.

Opposite: This glacial rock barn in Montana has been a local landmark for over a century and was placed on the National Register of Historic Places in 1977.

Photographs by Chuck Haney, Whitefish, Montana

Wine Country's Mysterious Round Barn:
Fountain Grove Barn, Santa Rosa, California

Sitting right next to California Highway 101 just north of Santa Rosa in Sonoma County is a curious round barn with a mysterious past and a secured future as a local landmark. The Fountain Grove barn has piqued the interest of historians ever since it rose up out of unusual circumstances more than a century ago. These circumstances included its location in the middle of a utopian community headed by Thomas Lake Harris. Harris, a mystic and writer, had brought a cult group called the Brotherhood of New Life west from New York state, where they had supported themselves as winemakers.

When they put down roots, literally and figuratively, in Santa Rosa in 1885, Harris built a three-story Victorian mansion surrounded by lavish gardens, which he called "The Commandery." While this may have seemed out of character for a group that professed to giving up their worldly possessions, Harris continued to preach an eclectic doctrine that blended several religious teachings and a lot of Eastern religions such as Shintoism.

One of the followers he attracted to his fold was Kenaye Nagasawa, a Samurai and young Japanese nobleman. When the brotherhood established a Fountain Grove winery complex, Nagasawa and a Missouri winemaker named Dr. John Hyde played leading roles. Within five years, the brotherhood had created a successful 2,000-acre vineyard and were shipping wine under the Fountain Grove label to distributors in London and New York. At one time, they produced 90 percent of the wine in Sonoma County, and the product was internationally acclaimed.

The idyllic Brotherhood of New Life suffered a meltdown in 1892, however, when the little community was rocked by sex scandals, and Harris and his wife fled California. Kenaye Nasagawa eventually inherited the entire estate and lived there quite comfortably as the colorful "Japanese Baron of Fountain Grove" until his death in 1934.

The sixteen-sided redwood barn was built by Nasagawa in 1899 to house the horses used at the winery and was fairly typical of round barns of the day. It had a central hayloft on the upper story, with stalls on the lower floor arranged in a circular pattern to shelter twenty-eight horses. The barn is about seventy feet in diameter and almost sixty feet high. With its distinctive architecture, open cupola, and attractively paired windows around the perimeter, it is a prominent attraction in this community today. Its unusual story is just another page of California wine country history.

Its distinctiveness and prime Santa Rosa location have marked the barn as a candidate for conversion to a restaurant.

Opposite: Although not truly round, this sixteen-sided barn in California's wine country was built in 1899 and is one of the oldest such on the West Coast. Truly round barns are usually constructed from small building blocks such as brick, since a wooden barn would ordinarily require too much shaping of the siding boards.

Along the Westward Trail:
California Ranch Barn, Mica, Washington

It was in 1867 that Henry Lueg's wagon train—following the "Kentuck Trail" en route to Portland, Oregon—stopped overnight at a ranch not far from the Spokane River in Washington. Fortunately for posterity, Henry kept a journal and described the ranch and the way station as "a house where some articles of necessity are to be had." He went on to explain that "intoxication drinks are sold at all the houses along the road, because most travelers have the idea that such drinks are necessary on the trips." Henry Lueg did not record the name of the owner of the ranch, but later sources identify him vaguely as a man named Knight. Little is known about Knight, except that he was a freighter who built the stopover on the Kentuck Trail and named it the "California Ranch" in memory of his days as a forty-niner in the California Gold Rush.

Much more is known, though, about the successor who bought out Knight's squatter's rights in 1871. Maxime Muloine, a French-Canadian who followed gold rushes from Canada to California, was one of the region's earliest pioneers and acquired property that covered more than fifteen square miles. Muloine had about 400 acres under cultivation by 1900, an unusually large ranch compared to the typical 160-acre homestead claims.

The California Ranch is the oldest continuously occupied farm or ranch in Spokane County, Washington, and was the only established ranch along the famous Kentuck Trail in the 1860s. As such, it was an important way station and resting place for hundreds of travelers: miners, hunters, packers, and early settlers who passed through this region during its frontier period. It prospered as a way station because Muloine took great pains to meet the needs of guests, even building a large rock wine cellar of hand-pitched stone.

At the center of the operation was a large bank barn that housed the teams of horses used by the many travelers who stopped at the ranch overnight. Still standing today, the circa 1864 structure is built against a sloping hillside that allows entry to all three of its different levels from the outside. The rectangular building, about fifty by ninety feet, has an upper level for hay storage, a working floor with wagon access, and a lower level used to house stock. A spring surfaces through the lower level's dirt floor, and the original well with hand pump is still in place. The registered historic site provides a tangible, visible remembrance of pioneer days in the Northwest.

Gathering rain clouds and this "greening" roof give a hint of wet weather that exists here much of the year.

In good repair today, the California Ranch barn is a valuable example of barns of the pioneer days.

Opposite: This old Washington state ranch and way station was a welcome sight for weary travelers in the 1860s. It was the only rest stop on a well-worn trail to Portland, Oregon.

Replacing Pieces of the Past:
Wilder Ranch Barns, Santa Cruz, California

"It's only in recent history that people have started to see the importance of barns in the life of the everyday man," says California state park ranger Steve Radesovich at Wilder Ranch State Park. "And that's kind of what you have here." What you have here, at the park outside Santa Cruz, is a historic central coast dairy ranch that includes, among other things, a cow barn dating back to the 1840s and an 1891 Victorian horse barn.

The Wilder Ranch is a state historical park cultural preserve and provides a faithful example of a ranch and dairy business dating back to 1859. It includes an original 1839 adobe, the Wilder family's 1896 Victorian home, granary, farmhouse, and other farm buildings. But the barns alone mark the preserve as a national treasure.

The crown jewel is undeniably the 1891 Victorian-style horse barn, considered one of the most ornate barns of the area. It is also one of the most fragile, and preservationists say that it will require considerable work, top to bottom, to arrest its decay and fully restore it. There are some favorable signs, though. In addition to a unique architectural design and five-color paint, the barn boasts one unexpected and enduring construction feature. The floor is macadam (a low-grade blacktop of oil and sand combined) that has been broken up, heated, and rolled out over a rock base. The result is a very durable flooring that allows the barn to continue to be used to shelter the ranch horses.

The Wilder Ranch cow barn is older by fifty years and has undergone some unusual expansion and contraction. In 1892, the original building was doubled in length to measure 36 feet wide and 300 feet long. The space was needed, too, in the 1920s, when the dairy was producing a ton of butter per day. By the 1950s, however, the dairy cows had been replaced by beef cattle and quarter horses, so the barn was reduced back to its original size. Even in the present truncated version, the dairy barn is a sight to behold.

The park's renewal is a long-term process. The Wilder Ranch began as a Spanish land grant 200 years ago and was in the Wilder family for five generations. It became a 4,500-acre state park in 1989 and is now embraced by preservationists and archaeologists as a model for restoration.

It's not a riddle, but the long cow barn today is the same length as the original structure but only half its former length.

A long-wearing macadam floor and design detail are hallmarks of the horse barn.

One of many barn swallows that have taken up residence in the historic north coast complex.

Opposite: The 1891 Victorian style horse barn at the Wilder Ranch has more than just a pretty face. It features an unusual asphalt floor that was well ahead of its time.

Barnstorming Northeastern Oregon:
Milton-Freewater Area Barns, Milton-Freewater, Oregon

Search 'til the cows come home, but you're not likely to find a cluster of more interesting barns than the fertile concentration tucked into the northeastern edge of Oregon, thirty miles from Pendleton and close by the state line with Washington. Milton-Freewater is the "Apple Capital of Oregon," but the apple of its eye is the historic Frazier Farmstead Museum and the preservation of a pioneer past. A passion for preservation manifests itself in a dedicated historical society, a delightful barn tour, and the 1997 showing here of the Smithsonian Institution's barn exhibit, an exhibit that drew 5,000 spectators over a two-month run. The magnificent barns in the area, mostly built in the early 1900s, are of varied architectural designs but serve as a seamless link to the community's past.

Exhibit A: The Frazier barn. This spruced-up structure sits on the site of a 320-acre homestead claim purchased in 1867 by William Samuel Frazier. The gambrel roof barn was completed in 1918 and was used mainly for carriage and riding horses, remaining in use into the 1960s for townspeople to stable and pasture their horses. The entire Frazier estate was later bequeathed to the community and opened to the public as the Frazier Farmstead Museum in 1984. The estate includes the farmhouse, originally built in 1892, the famed barn, and several outbuildings. It was placed on the National Register of Historic Places in 1986 and was part of the Smithsonian's *Barn Again! Celebrating an American Icon* exhibit.

Exhibit B: The Winn barn. This arch-roof barn was built for around $2,500, constructed of clear grain Douglas fir delivered for $11 per thousand foot. The owner, George Winn, hand-sawed every board that was used to build the barn, using his harvest crew in the spring and summer of 1916. Ground was cleared and a foundation laid in April, and the barn was completed for hay storage by harvest time. Half of the barn had ten stalls for horses, and the other half had twenty-five cow stanchions. In spite of its size and ambitious production schedule, the barn reflects a lot of detailing and precise work in windows and cupolas.

Exhibit C: The Cockburn barn. The high, rounded roofline accentuates the imposing size of this solitary sentinel. The barn was built in 1923 for $8,000 by Bill Carter, the son of owner Johnny Carter. It provided a hayloft above and housing for thirty-two mules, but tractors replaced the mules after only four years. It is now used primarily for storage.

The 1916 Winn barn boasts no posts in the entire structure.

Use of the Cockburn barn to house mules was short lived. They were replaced by tractors after only four years.

Opposite: The Frazier Farmstead barn, built in 1918, features an attractive exterior as well as interior details such as a unique central spiral staircase to the hayloft. This old time-traveler was cleaned out and wired up to host a modern-day Smithsonian exhibit.

The Dairy Barns of Marin County:
National Seashore Park, Point Reyes, California

The dairy barn was the last of the various types of American barn designs to become established, and writer Steve Bjerklie explains that "Prior to the Civil War, dairying was a very local business, so local, in fact, that a great deal of milk wound up in hog slop or in cheese because it could not be shipped or stored. But the emergence of national railroads, plus the development of the refrigerated railcar (which hugely benefited meatpackers, too) created a true dairy economy." With farmers given the option of raising large dairy herds and marketing all the milk produced, the big stall-lined dairy barn was born.

This didn't all happen in Wisconsin. Some of the most beautiful and innovative dairy barns in the country can be found along the majestic coastline in Marin County, California, north of San Francisco. The picturesque wave-washed Point Reyes coast is a far cry from the midwestern dairy scene, and so are the barns—mostly white, with "reverse gambrel" roof styles, prompting writer Bjerklie to characterize them as tending to be "wedges rather than humps, more ship than ark."

The era of the Point Reyes dairies began in 1857 but continues today with many of the old families still operating the dairies their fathers and grandfathers worked. Today, the ranches are under National Park Service management, which is dedicated to preserving their cultural heritage.

An imposing red barn near the park headquarters is, except for its color, a good example of the prevailing local style. Like other dairy barns, it was painted white in earlier days, but it was repainted prior to its purchase by the park in 1964. The fifty-two-by-ninety-eight-foot hay barn was built in 1870 as part of the Shafter/Howard dairy empire, a business so successful that by 1920 ranch trucks delivered 500 gallons of milk a day to San Francisco. The hay barn was remodeled in 1944 with new roofing and a concrete foundation, but it still has the original timber framing.

Another gem is the Pierce Point Ranch, established in 1858 by Solomon Pierce and now being restored by the the National Park Service as perhaps the best surviving example of a pioneer Point Reyes dairy. The ranch consists of eighteen buildings, dating from circa 1860 to 1933, and has been listed on the National Register of Historic Places.

The 1880s hay barn at Pierce Point Ranch features a shingled gable roof and a diamond-shaped window at the peak of its eastern gabled end.

The high ceiling, single window, and radiant light streaming through the siding yield a church-like aura to the Pierce barn interior.

The enduring interior of the Pierce barn masks the effects of over a hundred years of heavy use.

Opposite: This red hay barn, once painted white like other Marin dairy barns, sits at Point Reyes National Seashore in a Northern California area known for dairying since the mid-1800s. The "W" designation on the cupola was a letter given to the Bear Valley Ranch in the 1860s.

Why Are Barns Red?:
Barn Notes on Traditional Color

For almost 200 years, red has been the traditional color for American barns. That wasn't always the case. Prior to the 1700s, farmers were content to let the weather cure their barns. In the late 1700s, however, painting came into vogue in Virginia with the advent of colonial gray barns that took their ashen tones from lampblack.

A decade later, red barns began replacing the colonial grays. The red color was a derivative of ferrous oxide (rust), a common component of paint mixtures in New England because it was cheap and easily obtained. Mixed with skim milk and lime, the paint hardened into a protective coating that, when dried, resulted in the reddish hue. Eventually linseed oil was added to give the paint the ability to penetrate the wood. This became the standard, and the familiar red barn was born. (The red color was also used for many other industrial buildings of the time and was universally adopted for early railroads. In fact, the brick color was commonly called "boxcar red" or "caboose red.")

Aside from a few heretics—such as dairy barn owners who prefer the sanitary look of a white barn—barns are generally associated with the color red. With the array of quality paints offered today and the broad spectrum of colors available, one might wonder why red continues to be the preferred color. Aside from the tug of tradition, only one other theory has emerged. Some years ago, a DuPont colorist advanced a proposition based on behavioral science that farmers suffered from "red starvation" because of the preponderance of greenery in their environment. Apparently, the red color in barns and outbuildings helps alleviate the sensory imbalance and restores equilibrium to their rural surroundings. The jury is still out, but to most observers "a barn is a barn is a barn," and red remains the traditional color.

Many coats of bright red paint have kept this 1894 California barn proud and protected.

The unfinished old wooden barn and its new red successor provide an interesting study in contrasts on a back road near Glenoma, Washington.

Pigments may come and go, but "barn red" continues to lead all other colors in the painting of farm buildings.

Opposite: A splash of red seen through a curtain of greenery, a common color combination on this country road in southwestern Idaho. Photograph © by Ken Levy, Photographer's Art Galleries, www.kenlevymedia.com

The Untold Stories in No-Name Barns:
Barn Notes on Anonymous Western Barns

When a passerby was asked about the particulars and "story" of an abandoned barn, he said simply, "That barn don't have a story." We all know better. Every barn has a story … we just may not know it.

The same might have been said of the story told by Barbara, a California housewife, about "Granddad's barn." She said her most cherished early memories were of visits to her grandfather's farm in Colorado. One particular memory, though, she kept hushed for forty years.

It seems that on that visit, the grandfather made the barn off limits because his prize beagle was in heat and he had temporarily confined her to the hayloft. The dog was to remain there until a trip into town where she would be bred by a suitable male beagle. (He specifically wanted to keep her safe from Zac, a hot-blooded little fox terrier who ruled the barnyard.) Naturally, five-year-old Barbara didn't understand such things, so she climbed the ladder to the loft—with Zac under her arm. While Barb explored the place, Zac and the beagle attended to nature's business. Later, Barbara tired of the loft, returned Zac to the barnyard, and ran off to other pursuits. The visit to the barn loft was never mentioned.

You can imagine, then, Granddad's shock two months later when his prize beagle gave birth to a curious litter of black-and-white spotted pups bearing a strong terrier resemblance. Scratching his head in amazement, he said, "How in the hell did that terrier get up there?" No one ever told him, and for months afterward he claimed to have the only dog in the county who could climb a vertical nine-foot ladder.

A no-name barn in Tierra Amarillo, New Mexico.

Who, me? Could a terrier climb a barn ladder?

Two curious bystanders at an unidentified barn in Williams, California.

Opposite: This unidentified great barn in Meridian, Idaho, has an inviting appearance and suggests many untold stories. Photograph © by Ken Levy, Photographer's Art Galleries, www.kenlevymedia.com

Weather Report:

Continuous and Destructive: Barn Notes on Weather

In a standoff between wood and the elements, the rain, snow, wind, and sun usually win. At least that's the case in these images of weathered wooden barns of the West. Even redwood eventually must come to terms with the weather.

Take the example on the facing page. This "falling-down barn" near Donnelly, Idaho, has reached a point of no return, but the old leaner resists lying down on the job. The other pictorial examples here are no less distressing. When a New Mexico farm building's unprotected wooden siding began to yield, the battle was apparently joined by tar paper, but that was also eventually ripped away. The battered barn near Granada, California, is barely hanging on, and the roof of a crumpled barn in southwest Idaho sags from its share of hard times and hard weather.

We know that much of the hardwood in the West can withstand harsh wind and weather in its unfinished state. And, in some cases, it isn't the fault of the timber, but faulty design or construction that causes a barn to tilt or collapse. Appearances are also deceiving, and sometimes a barn appearing on the verge of collapse can hang on for many years.

Despite a trend to metal barns and prefabs that are delivered right to their foundations, purists won't accept anything but natural wood. For a first-quality barn, they say, demand first-quality wood. A whimsical story, however, illustrates the wrong way to go about it. It seems that a good Catholic man went to confession, telling the priest that he worked in a lumberyard and confessing that over the years he often "took pieces of wood" home with him at night.

The priest, thinking it was not a serious misdeed, asked the man how much wood he had taken home. "Well," said the man, "enough to build a new barn for my brother's farm." The priest was shocked. He reasoned that this was far too serious to just dispense simple penance and that the sinner needed to get away and take time to meditate on his transgressions. "My son," the priest said, "Have you ever thought about a retreat?" The man quickly and enthusiastically replied, "No, Father, but if you've got the plans, I can get the wood!"

A battered barn near Granada, California, has less-than-golden prospects for the future.

Cattle are unconcerned about the sagging roof of this barn in Kuna, Idaho.

This barn near Mayhill, New Mexico, lost its siding and tar paper topcoat to wind and weather.

Visitors Unwelcome:
Barn Notes on Property Protection

Locating historic out-of-the-way farm buildings is difficult enough for photographers and barn lovers, but the task becomes next to impossible when a farm owner prefers that the buildings remain unnoticed and undisturbed.

Sometimes it's for their own good, since visitors have stripped many an old barn or outbuilding of its weathered wood, often to use in crafts. (The wood has become scarce enough that serious owners who are presently restoring historic barns report difficulty finding appropriate weathered wood to match.) One historian suspects that the advent of jeeps after World War II plus the later boom in off-road vehicles brought a lot of tourists into backwoods areas where once-forgotten farm buildings, signs, and fence posts became easy prey for souvenir hunters.

Oftentimes when a tourist, barn seeker or not, ventures into a small rural town, he may find his presence either ignored or unwelcome by the locals. You can't blame residents for being unhappy about outsiders poking around and disturbing the tranquility of the place.

One such tourist in a hot sports car screeched to a stop outside the general store and asked an old man on the porch several inane questions about the area. As he prepared to pull out, he concluded by asking, "What's the speed limit in this place?" "We don't have any," replied the old man, "we like for you folks to get through here just as fast as possible!"

This abandoned turn-of-the-century barn near the entrance to Utah's Zion National Park is inviting to visitors, well intentioned or otherwise.

Visitors might get the impression that they are unwelcome at this Julian, California, location.

Early morning sun exposes the stripped skeleton of an old barn near Capay, California.

Opposite: The circa 1900 Herrin family barn near Donnelly, Idaho, is tempting to souvenir hunters. Photograph © by Ken Levy, Photographer's Art Galleries, www.kenlevymedia.com

93

Barn Styles:

Historic Barns Reflect Ethnic Traditions, Local Customs, and a Changing Society

American barns have been called "vernacular architecture" by historians … simple structures that reflect local and regional traditions. This makes it difficult to separate any barn from the people and the history of the land, and even more difficult to categorize a "western barn," which is often a combination of earlier eastern barn styles that have been adapted to the particular needs of an owner. Since few older barns were built to standardized plans, the individual style often became the product of the builder's experience and personal preferences, with a nod to prevailing styles of the region.

Aside from regional similarities, though, each barn has a unique fingerprint, one that is a little different from any other barn. While the most evident identifier may be its overall shape or roof style, the building also bears other less-obvious characteristics. Such nuances may reflect the origin and ethnicity of its builder, kind of animals housed there, nature of the farm's crops, available building materials, woodworking craftsmanship, unusual construction techniques, and necessary accommodations to terrain and weather, to name but a few. As writer Steve Bjerklie has said, "In no common structure are the qualities of form and function interlocked more eloquently and beautifully than in the barn."

In examining the history of an old barn, one cannot help but also uncover bits and pieces of American history, our agricultural heritage, and those who shaped it. This is a nation of immigrants, and the evolving barn styles kindled by the European pioneers on the eastern seaboard found their way, with certain changes, into the barns of the West.

Although "standard" barn designs and plans were available in farm magazines of the mid-1800s, for the most part, our American barns were homemade by local craftsmen to fit the specific needs of a specific farm. Only a handful were designed by architects. Barns of the time were largely built from materials found in the immediate area—log construction, sealed with mud or straw. These were simple boxlike buildings along the lines of the English barn. The arrivals in the 1680s of German settlers in Pennsylvania and the Dutch in New York brought new bigger barn designs that became the model to be followed for many years. These barns were large two-story structures with a hayloft over a ground floor that contained a working (threshing) area and stalls for livestock. The interior structural design was characterized by mortised, tenoned, and pegged beams arranged in H-shaped units with columned aisles alongside a central workspace. The H frames were connected by timbers running the length of the barn.

The Western Barn

The long, sweeping roof is a characteristic of the western barn. Typically, the building had to provide large storage space for hay and feed, and the shape and extended roof accommodated this need. It has great similarities with the Dutch barn and also is seen with many variations of roof styles, broken and unbroken. The saltbox, or "catslide," roof, for instance, features a longer sloping roof on the side facing the prevailing wind. Some western barns are also reminiscent of double crib barns, in that they sheltered cattle on one side and horses on the other, with a driveway, work, or storage area in the center.

Opposite: This 1918 vestle barn near Genessee, Idaho, suggests an inverted ship. Were it in the Southwest, that would not be so far fetched. In the late 1800s, some New Mexico barns were built by a traveling band of Scandinavian boatbuilders. Photograph © by Ken Levy, Photographer's Art Galleries, www.kenlevymedia.com

One clever innovation by German settlers was the ingenious addition of a third story. By building the barn into the bank of a hill, the lower level for animals was sheltered by the slope itself, and the Pennsylvania "bank barn" could be entered at the second level by wagons bearing wheat or hay.

Over the years, other style variations came into being: crib barns in the South and Southeast, adobe barns in the Southwest, and a smattering of round barns popularized countrywide in the late 1800s (George Washington built one over a hundred years earlier). As farming and ranching spread west of the Rockies, the emerging barn styles there included many of the eastern prototypes, as well as combinations of different styles.

After 1900, style became secondary to survival. The future for barns faced severe challenges in the twentieth century as the family farm began to disappear. Farmers who previously raised varied crops and livestock for their own use turned to commercial farming, often with only one or two crops. As farming became more specialized, many farms with multipurpose barns gave way to specialized barns that had to be adapted to new requirements (or replaced with uninteresting metal prefabs). The number of older barns declined and continues to decline, while various new uses and styles have increased. Although dwindling in number today, the remaining historic western barns, circa 1900 or earlier, hold increased allure for historians. The years have added interest to their stories, their early beginnings, and their implausible survival.

One nagging question has remained unclear—just what is a "western barn"? Like its predecessor, the prairie barn, it was originally somewhat larger than midwestern barns because of the greater need for storage space associated with larger herds. In the typical stockman's barn configuration, one can also see the traces of the Dutch barn—the long rooflines, the doors in the gabled end, and the positioning of stalls in aisles on either side of a work or storage area. Another common western barn is a modification of the old crib barn, with a tall middle section that is distinct from the wings on either side. The western barn takes many shapes, though—too many to yield much consensus on which western barn is the prototype. It is difficult to generalize when covering a canvas as wide as the West—from the Pacific Northwest to New Mexico, with extreme terrain and weather differences in between.

Bank Barns

The bank barn, also called the Pennsylvania bank barn, is built into the side of a hill, permitting two levels to be entered from the ground. The lower level housed animals, and the upper levels served as threshing floor and storage. The earthen ramp of the hillside entrance made easy second-level access possible to wagons transporting wheat or hay, and stored feed could be dropped from that level to the animals below. A distinguishing feature is the projecting upper level, or forebay. This second level was often extended, or cantilevered, over the first, and the overhang sheltered animals from the inclement weather and allowed feed to be dropped directly to the outside.

Opposite: The Moulton barn, in Wyoming's Grand Teton National Park, was begun in 1913 on Mormon Row, a three-mile lane homesteaded by a dozen Mormon families. Most of the homesteaded land, including the barn, now belongs to the National Park Service. It reflects a combination of the typical characteristics of western barns. Photograph © by Ken Levy, Photographer's Art Galleries, www.kenlevymedia.com

Dutch Barns

The barns built by early Dutch settlers of New York state were characterized by the broad gable roof and doors for wagons in the narrow (gabled) end. A pent roof (or pentice) over the center door gave some slight protection from the elements. The siding is typically horizontal, and there were few openings in the exterior walls other than the doors. The heavy interior structural system is a distinctive feature of the Dutch barn. Mortised, tenoned, and pegged beams are arranged in H-shaped units that resemble a church interior, with columned aisles alongside a central space.

For definition's sake, though, we can say that traditional western barns are generally of simple design and wooden construction. They are usually of redwood or lodgepole pine, woods that do quite well without paint and, over time, acquire a gray, weathered look that can make them look older than their actual years.

The form of the barn usually features a peak roof over a hayloft and a long sweeping roof—sometimes flatter than other roofs because snow load is not as great a factor. The barn may have a straight, uniformly sloped roof, or it may have a higher middle section and two wings on either side. In some cases, the shed roofs of the wings will not reach the top of the middle section's walls, thus leaving space for small clerestory windows. A traditional western barn typically has stalls for livestock on either side of a central work and storage area.

Milder weather in much of the West permits livestock to remain outdoors year-round, so cattle barns can be smaller. The simple shed roof has likely replaced the gambrel roof since hay storage is not so critical for animals foraging outside. Nevertheless, there are some enormous hay barns in cattle country that exist only to store hay and simple horse barns used primarily for storing fodder and providing part-time shelter for horses in bad weather.

The more-or-less "typical" barns of the western United States do not preclude many other styles and variations. Gothic roof barns appear unexpectedly from time to time, as do even ornate Victorian and Italianate barns, as well as weathered old adobe and stone structures. The examples of historic barns throughout this book underscore the variety and versatility of this unique "vernacular architecture" and demonstrate that barns of the West add considerably to the rich tradition of American farm buildings.

Crib Barns

Crib barns, found throughout the South and Southeast, are an important genre of American barns. This style is constructed of one or more cribs, the cribs serving as storage for fodder (or pens for livestock). A typical double-crib barn has two cribs, with a central driveway between to allow a team and wagon to pass through the barn after unloading. Crib barns may or may not have a hayloft above, but in larger double-crib barns, a second-story hayloft is sometimes cantilevered over the ground floor, resulting in a barn of striking appearance.

Round Barns

The heyday of round barns was from 1880 until around 1920 and was spurred by their promise of increased efficiency. The circular form offered greater volume-to-surface ratio than a rectangular or square form, providing lower material costs and greater storage space. Animal stalls were arranged around a central manger, and hay was dropped down from above. The claims were overstated, however, and the round or multisided barn never became a standard style, although many were built across the country. There were some significant design problems not present in conventional barn construction, as well as dealing with unusual stall shapes and space allocation.

Darrell Newton, of Nashville, Michigan, employed a barn trussing technique to convert an 1895 dairy/hay barn to new uses. Before renovation, Newton had to store his wagons, grain drill, tractors, plows, and corn planter outside all winter. The innovative project created an open-span building for machinery storage and a work area, and it increased usable space by more than 20,000 square feet while still leaving room for a renovated haymow and saving $7,000 over a comparable new building. "It would have been a big waste to bulldoze the barn just because it didn't fit my needs," said Newton, who received a National Trust award of merit for the project.

Preservation and the Barn Again! Program:
National Efforts to Preserve Historic Farm Buildings

And the barn was a witness, stood and saw it all.
—Carl Sandburg, from *The People, Yes*

When the National Trust for Historic Preservation and *Successful Farming* magazine launched the Barn Again! program in 1987, historic barns were considered doomed. The exodus from the farm to the cities, which actually began in the mid-1800s, had taken its toll on the population of historic farm buildings. The changing face of American agriculture in the 1900s also brought into question the feasibility of keeping old barns that no longer provided adequate storage. Obsolete for modern farming needs and too expensive to maintain as family heirlooms, old barns appeared destined to be preserved only in photographs and memories.

The Barn Again! program has not totally reversed the trend, but it has certainly exerted a strong influence upon it. The National Trust for Historic Preservation, a national organization that protects America's significant old buildings, saw the need not only to preserve barns, but also to restore them and return them to productive use. Hundreds of success stories later, the Barn Again! program has shown how historic barns can be adapted for new farming uses ranging from dairy, hog, and cattle operations to machinery or grain storage. Barn preservation techniques have proven to be cost-effective alternatives to tearing down the old barn and putting up a new building. (While Barn Again! stresses restoring the structures for agricultural use, other organizations have joined the cause, pursuing end-uses such as homes, restaurants, art galleries, and museums.)

The Barn Again! program provides advice, information, and referrals to barn owners, including technical guides on reconstruction, awards for preserving historic rural resources, financing options, workshops, and traveling exhibits. They work with partners to develop state and local barn preservation programs and have fueled special projects such as the popular Public Television program *Barn Again!: Celebrating the Restoration of Historic Farm Buildings* and the traveling exhibit by the Smithsonian Institution *Barn Again!: Celebrating an American Icon.*

The prospects for barn preservation have brightened considerably, but the ultimate decision rests in the hands of barn owners. While aging barns are sometimes converted into houses or for non-farming purposes, it is reassuring to see many of them being rehabilitated and put back to productive agricultural work. There are, at least, a number of alternative answers now to the question, "What can you do with that old barn?" Options include farm shop, machinery storage, hog farrowing, grain storage, cold-weather livestock shelter, residence, meeting hall, and barn dance hall, to name a few. Today, there are plenty of resources available to help barn owners make those important restoration decisions.

The Barn Again! program is headquartered at the Denver, Colorado, regional office of the National Trust. For more information, contact:

Barn Again!
National Trust for Historic Preservation
535 16th Street, Suite 750
Denver, CO 80202
(303) 623-1504
www.barnagain.org

This 1870 cattle/hay barn in Knoxville, Illinois, was slip sliding away—with sagging walls, crumbling stones, and a foundation slowly sinking into the ground. But, in a Barn Again! demonstration project, farmer Janis King added a rebuilt foundation and other repairs and now has a very serviceable bank barn at a savings of $25,000 over an equivalent new barn. She not only saved the barn, but also a valuable piece of the community's agricultural heritage.

The Cooper barn, touted as the largest barn in Kansas, was built in 1936 as a cattle barn for Hereford show cattle and later also housed mules and Clydesdale horses. When the declining farm was sold, the barn was donated to the Thomas County Historical Society in 1991, "if it could be moved" to a Prairie Museum site some sixteen miles away. Like a story right out of "Believe It or Not," the irrepressible historical group raised the money and moved the 150-ton barn intact—standing 48 feet tall and measuring 114 feet by 66 feet! After its incredible relocation and restoration, the Cooper barn is now a major attraction at the Prairie Museum of Art and History in Colby, Kansas, containing the museum's agricultural exhibit and serving as the site of many barn dances and special events.

Acknowledgments

This book would not have been possible, at least not in its present scope and detail, without the assistance of many dedicated volunteers. These good folk unselfishly gave of their time to preserve a heritage they deemed worth saving. We are grateful to you and your organizations.

Research Assistance

Dorothy Victor, New Mexico Office of Cultural Affairs, Santa Fe, New Mexico; Julie Brooks, Wickenburg Chamber of Commerce, Wickenburg, Arizona; Mella Rothwell Harmon, Nevada State Historic Preservation Office; Zee Hill, Greg Griffith, and staff, Washington State Office of Historic Preservation; Marilyn McCray, Ojo Caliente Mineral Springs, New Mexico.

Paul Taylor, historian, Mesilla, New Mexico; Elvis Fleming, Historical Center for Southeast New Mexico, Roswell, New Mexico; Nancy A. Niedernhofer, Oregon State Historic Preservation Office; Chelsea Pickslay, California Historical Society, San Francisco, California; Beverly Pirtle, Dona Ana County Historical Society, Las Cruces, New Mexico; Charles Leik, editor of *The Barn Journal*, www.thebarnjournal.org; John Olson, Barn Again! program, National Trust for Historic Preservation; Steve Bjerklie, Point Reyes Station, California; Alice Dove, Kleffner Ranch, Montana; Frazier Farmstead Museum, Milton-Freewater, Oregon; Connie Brumback, Harney County, Oregon Chamber of Commerce.

Barn owners and custodians of western history who nourished our mind and spirit and provided valuable background information: Martha Steinke Dechenne, Paula Hanson, Bob and Linda Hemborg, Roy Hendricks, Jill and Rob Van Daalen, Ed Preston and Dogie Jones.

Photo Credits

We wish to thank the following photo contributors who shared their work with us.
Ken Levy Photography: www.kenlevymedia.com (pages 38–39, 60–61, 86, 88, 90–94, 96) Copyright 2003; © Jack Hursh Photos, Reno, Nevada (pages viii, x, 6, 7); © Deane P. Lewis, www.owlpages.com (page 51); Casey T. Murawski, Richmond, Utah (page 14); O.K. Corral, Tombstone, Arizona: Virginia Hatfield, Erik Hinote, Robert Love (pages 28–29); Ed and Sheila Preston, Preston Farms (page 45); The Flying E Ranch, Wickenburg, AZ (page 54); Historical Center for Southeast New Mexico, John Chisum photo (page 37); Interpretation & Educational Division, Photographic Archives, California State Parks 2001 (page 9); The First American Corporation, Irvine, California (page 53); John Olson, National Trust for Historic Preservation, and John Walter, *Successful Farming* magazine (pages 18–19, 62–63, 69, 100, 102); Stanford University News Service (pages 46–47); Prairie Museum of Art and History, Colby, Kansas (page 103); Chuck Haney Photography, Whitefish. Montana (pages 74–75); Dogie Jones, Watrous, New Mexico (pages 58–59); Carolyn Graham photography, Roswell, New Mexico (page 36); Earnie Moran, Moran's Photography, Brewster, Washington (page 44); Don Baccus, dhogaza@pacifier.com, Portland, Oregon (page 3); Bob Gibson, Blue Water Photo, Lincoln City, Oregon (page 2); Historic Preservation Division, State of New Mexico Office of Cultural Affairs (page 16).